Math Skills Workout

Grade 5

About This Book

Your friends at *The Mailbox®* have done it again! We've combined four previously published books of *The Mailbox* Math Series for Grade 5 *(Problem Solving; Geometry; Measurement;* and *Probability, Statistics, & Graphing)* and added a completely new section on algebra. This new compilation—*Math Skills Workout Grade 5*—offers everything you need in one book to reinforce math concepts with your students.

The two-page activities in *Math Skills Workout Grade 5* are designed to reinforce previously introduced math concepts. Each activity has a colorful teacher page and a skill-based reproducible student page.

The teacher page includes the following:
- the purpose of the activity
- a summary of what students will do
- a list of all needed materials, including any provided patterns
- vocabulary to review before the students complete the reproducible
- two fun-filled extension activities

The student page is a skill-based reproducible that supports NCTM standards. Each reproducible has a bonus box designed to provide an extra challenge. Answer keys are provided in the back of the book.

Select from the variety of activities to meet your students' individual needs. Then use the accompanying extension activities to provide extra skill reinforcement or to informally assess students' progress. Tailoring math practice has never been so easy!

www.themailbox.com

More great math books from *The Mailbox*®

Writer: Ann Snider
Project Manager: Peggy W. Hambright
Copy Editors: Gina Farago, Karen Brewer Grossman, Karen L. Huffman, Amy Kirtley, Debbie Shoffner
Cover Artist: Clevell Harris
Art Coordinator: Clevell Harris
Artists: Pam Crane, Teresa R. Davidson, Theresa Lewis Goode, Nick Greenwood, Clevell Harris, Sheila Krill, Clint Moore, Barry Slate
Typesetters: Lynette Maxwell, Mark Rainey

President, The Mailbox Book Company™: Joseph C. Bucci
Book Development Managers: Stephen Levy, Elizabeth H. Lindsay, Thad McLaurin, Susan Walker
Book Planning Manager: Chris Poindexter
Curriculum Director: Karen P. Shelton
Traffic Manager: Lisa K. Pitts
Librarian: Dorothy C. McKinney
Editorial and Freelance Management: Karen A. Brudnak
Editorial Training: Irving P. Crump
Editorial Assistants: Terrie Head, Melissa B. Montanez, Hope Rodgers, Jan E. Witcher

©2001 THE EDUCATION CENTER, INC.
All rights reserved.
ISBN #1-56234-462-5

Manufactured in the United States

10 9 8 7 6 5 4 3 2 1

Table of Contents

Measurement

Geometry

Probability, Statistics, and Graphing

Algebra

Problem Solving

Perfectly Suited for Space

Try some metric measurement practice that's truly out of this world!

Purpose: To complete measurements to the nearest centimeter

Students will do the following:

- estimate the length of body measurements to the nearest centimeter
- measure the length of body measurements to the nearest centimeter
- calculate the difference between the estimates and measurements
- calculate the mean for the measurements

Materials for each student:

- copy of page 6
- pencil
- string, 1.5–2 meters long
- centimeter ruler
- calculator (optional)

Vocabulary to review:

- centimeter
- estimate
- mean
- median
- mode
- range

Extension activities to use after the reproducible:

- Search out accurate measurement skills with a classroom scavenger hunt. Ahead of time, measure eight to ten classroom items to the nearest centimeter. Provide students with a list of these items. Then have students work in pairs to locate and measure the items to the nearest centimeter. As a challenge, include a few mystery items on the list. To do this, list the measurements for two or three mystery items but do not list the names of the items. Instruct each pair to locate an item in the class that is approximately the same size as one of the mystery items listed and then measure it to the nearest centimeter to see if they have correctly located a mystery item.

- Pencil in some more measurement practice with this activity. Have small groups of students estimate the length of each group member's pencil. Then ask students to measure the pencils. Have them compute the mean, median, mode, and range for their group's data. If desired, collect this data and compute the mean, median, mode, and range of the class's pencils.

Perfectly Suited for Space

Congratulations! You have been selected to fly on the next space shuttle mission! Before you can depart, NASA needs to make your space suit. To get a good fit, you'll need to supply some body measurements. Working in small groups, first estimate each measurement indicated below to the nearest centimeter. Then use string to measure from 1 point to another. Compare the string to your ruler to calculate the actual measurements to the nearest centimeter. Finally, determine the difference between the estimate and the measurement.

Height—Measure from the top of your head to the floor.
estimate: _____
actual: _____
difference: _____

Hat size—Measure around your head, just above your eyebrows.
estimate: _____
actual: _____
difference: _____

Arm span—Spread your arms out wide and measure from fingertip to fingertip.
estimate: _____
actual: _____
difference: _____

Neck—Measure around the thickest part of your neck.
estimate: _____
actual: _____
difference: _____

Waist to ankle—Measure from your waist to the bony point of your ankle.
estimate: _____
actual: _____
difference: _____

Waist—Measure the smallest part of your waist.
estimate: _____
actual: _____
difference: _____

Ankle—Measure the distance around your ankle.
estimate: _____
actual: _____
difference: _____

Foot length—Measure the longest part of your foot.
estimate: _____
actual: _____
difference: _____

Guess what! Your team members are going on the same space shuttle mission as you are! Work together to calculate the group's mean for the following measurements. When you're done, complete and cut out your space shuttle ticket below. You're ready to fly!

Mean hat size: _____
Mean arm span: _____
Mean foot length: _____
Mean height: _____

Bonus Box: Compute the median, mode, and range of team members' foot lengths.

Metric measurement is a blast! I'm all suited up for a ride on the space shuttle!

Astronaut's name: _____

Blastoff date: _____

Landing date: _____

Digging Into Your Desk

Make a clean sweep of customary measurement with an activity that's good, clean fun.

Purpose: To practice measurements to the nearest $\frac{1}{2}$, $\frac{1}{4}$, and $\frac{1}{8}$ inch

Students will do the following:

- measure pictures of school supplies to the nearest $\frac{1}{2}$, $\frac{1}{4}$, and $\frac{1}{8}$ inch

Materials for each student:

- copy of page 8
- pencil
- customary ruler

Vocabulary to review:

- $\frac{1}{2}$ inch
- $\frac{1}{4}$ inch
- $\frac{1}{8}$ inch

Extension activities to use after the reproducible:

- Have students dig deeply into their own desks to find items to measure. Challenge them to see how many items they can find that measure to exactly $\frac{1}{2}$, $\frac{1}{4}$, and $\frac{1}{8}$ inch. Ask for a show of hands to see which students think their desks are clean enough to be in Mr. Neatnik's class at Squeaky Clean Elementary.

- Add some art to your math lesson with this extension. Provide each student with construction paper in the following sizes: two 4" x 12" pieces, one 2" x 12" piece, and one 8" x 12" piece. Have each student measure and cut one piece of 4" x 12" paper into $\frac{1}{2}$-inch strips; the other piece of 4" x 12" paper into $\frac{1}{4}$-inch strips; and the piece of 2" x 12" paper into $\frac{1}{8}$-inch strips. Challenge the student to use the remaining 8" x 12" piece as the base and the strips to create 3-D artwork.

Digging Into Your Desk

It's the annual Desk-Cleaning Day at Squeaky Clean Elementary School. As Mr. Neatnik's fifth graders empty their desks, they are finding many objects that they can use to practice measuring to the nearest $\frac{1}{2}$, $\frac{1}{4}$, and $\frac{1}{8}$ inch. Below are some of those objects. Measure each as indicated to the nearest $\frac{1}{2}$, $\frac{1}{4}$, and $\frac{1}{8}$ inch.

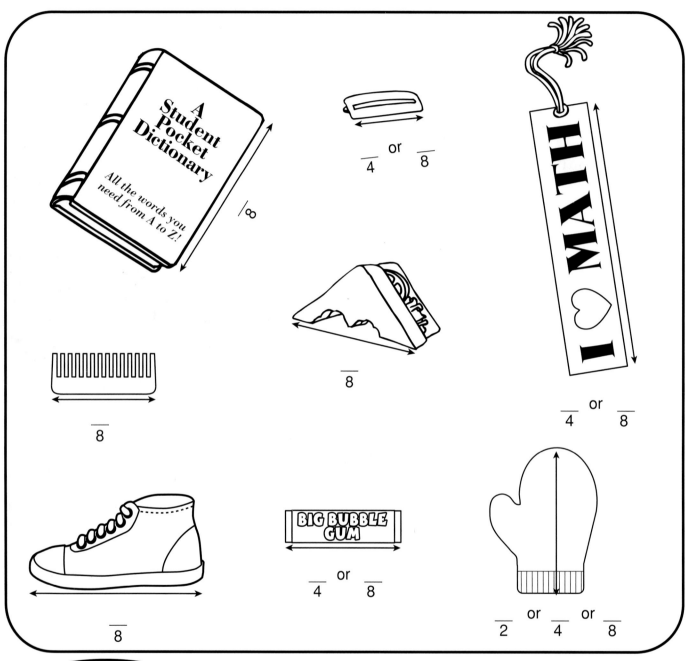

Mr. Neatnik's students aren't very neat and tidy, are they? Draw a line from the trash can to any item that these squeaky clean kids need to take home or throw away!

Bonus Box: Find 2 measurements above that you can add together to get a whole number.

Measuring Mass Is a Picnic in the Park

Show your students how measuring mass in metrics can be a picnic with this reproducible activity!

Purpose: To choose reasonable measurements of metric mass

Students will do the following:

- choose an appropriate measurement among milligrams, grams, and kilograms

Materials for each student:

- copy of page 10
- pencil

Vocabulary to review:

- milligrams
- grams
- kilograms

Extension activities to use after the reproducible:

- Divide your students into small groups. Supply each group with one metric scale and a set of small items, such as a pencil, an eraser, a crayon, a piece of chalk, and a glue stick. Instruct each group to predict the mass of each item from lightest to heaviest. Then have each group measure for exact mass and record its data on a sheet of paper. Next, have each group report its findings to the rest of the class. Have groups compare data for each object and present reasons why some items that appear to be the same may have different masses. *(For example, one team's glue stick may weigh less than another team's glue stick because it contains less glue.)*

- Have students combine their artistic talents with their knowledge of metric units of mass. Give each student two sheets of poster board, a supply of old magazines, scissors, glue, and a black marker. Instruct each student to label the top of one poster "Grams." Then have him label the top of the other poster "Kilograms." Next, instruct each student to look through the old magazines and cut out photographs and illustrations of items that are measured in grams and kilograms. Then have the student arrange and glue the cutouts on the appropriate sheets of poster board to create two collages—one for items measured in grams and one for items measured in kilograms. Hang the collages around the room or in a hallway during your study of metric mass.

Measuring Mass Is a Picnic in the Park

Measuring mass is a picnic in the park! Complete the activities below to show just how much you know about measuring using milligrams, grams, and kilograms.

Part I: Circle the most reasonable unit of measurement for each item shown below.

 1.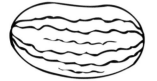

watermelon

milligram   gram   kilogram

 2.

ant

milligram   gram   kilogram

3.

photo album

milligram   gram   kilogram

 4.

Frisbee®

milligram   gram   kilogram

5.

cherry pie

milligram   gram   kilogram

 6.

jar of mustard

milligram   gram   kilogram

Part II: For each item listed below, circle the letter to the right that is in the column of the most reasonable unit of measurement for the item. Then write each circled letter in the appropriate numbered blank at the bottom of the page to help you find the answer to the following riddle: *What did the salad shout when the picnic food was ready?*

Item	mg	g	kg
1. horseshoe	A	L	P
2. raindrop	L	N	O
3. picnic table	I	U	E
4. volleyball	R	A	M
5. paper plate	P	S	T
6. bottle of soda	F	L	E
7. bowl of potato salad	M	H	L
8. dash of pepper	E	P	N

Item	mg	g	kg
9. bottle of ketchup	U	T	C
10. hot dog	I	T	O
11. piece of charcoal	S	U	G
12. grill	V	B	C
13. softball	D	E	J
14. wooden bat	K	Q	E
15. dab of sunscreen	A	V	S
16. watermelon seed	T	M	B

3 1833 04159 8811

___ ___ ___ ___ ___ ___ ___ ___ ___ ___ ___ ___ ___   ___ ___ ___!
 1   2   3   4   5   6   7   8   9 10 11 12 13   14 15 16

Bonus Box: On the back of this page, brainstorm 2 more picnic or food items for each unit of measurement—milligrams, grams, and kilograms.

Fishing Your "Weigh" Through Pounds and Ounces

Help your students catch on to converting pounds to ounces and vice versa with this activity!

Purpose: To convert standard capacity units of measurement

Students will do the following:

- convert ounces to pounds
- convert pounds to ounces
- identify heaviest and lightest weights
- calculate the total sum of given weights

Materials for each student:

- copy of page 12
- pencil

Vocabulary to review:

- convert
- ounces
- pounds
- total

Extension activities to use after the reproducible:

- Further extend your students' practice with renaming standard capacity units of measurement with this small-group or center activity. Collect various grocery items, such as a can of soup, box of pasta, bag of chips, etc. Tape a construction paper flap over the weight printed on each item. Have students estimate each item's weight and then arrange them from the heaviest to the lightest on a table. Then have students lift the flap covering each item's weight to see if they have correctly ordered the items.

- Give students more experience with renaming standard capacity units of measurement by holding a backpack weight contest. Obtain a pair of bathroom or balanced scales. Then have each student weigh her backpack in pounds. Then challenge each student to use the information on page 12 to help her convert the weight of her backpack to ounces. Give the students with the lightest and the heaviest backpacks a small treat.

Fishing Your "Weigh" Through Pounds and Ounces

Gus Grizzly and his buddies held a contest to see who could catch the heaviest fish! Complete the activities below to help Gus and his friends decide the winner of the contest.

Part I: Beside each bear is a list of each fish he caught and its weight. In the blanks provided, write the weight of each fish in order from heaviest to lightest.

16 ounces = 1 pound

Gus

Weight of Fish
Fish #1 = 32 ounces
Fish #2 = 1 pound 7 ounces
Fish #3 = 25 ounces
Fish #4 = 2 pounds 2 ounces
Fish #5 = 12 ounces
Fish #6 = 35 ounces

Garth

Weight of Fish
Fish #1 = 18 ounces
Fish #2 = 1 pound 8 ounces
Fish #3 = 2 pounds 1 ounce
Fish #4 = 29 ounces
Fish #5 = 15 ounces
Fish #6 = 1 pound 10 ounces

____ ____ ____ ____ ____ ____
Heaviest   Lightest

____ ____ ____ ____ ____ ____
Heaviest   Lightest

Gary

Weight of Fish
Fish #1 = 20 ounces
Fish #2 = 1 pound 10 ounces
Fish #3 = 1 pound 5 ounces
Fish #4 = 25 ounces
Fish #5 = 16 ounces
Fish #6 = 8 ounces

Gunther

Weight of Fish
Fish #1 = 2 pounds 2 ounces
Fish #2 = 27 ounces
Fish #3 = 17 ounces
Fish #4 = 1 pound 9 ounces
Fish #5 = 23 ounces
Fish #6 = 33 ounces

____ ____ ____ ____ ____ ____
Heaviest   Lightest

____ ____ ____ ____ ____ ____
Heaviest   Lightest

Part II: Use the information in Part I to help you answer the questions below.

1. How much did each bear's heaviest fish weigh in ounces? Pounds?

Gus _____ ounces
_____ pound(s) _____ ounce(s)

Garth _____ ounces
_____ pound(s) _____ ounce(s)

Gary _____ ounces
_____ pound(s) _____ ounce(s)

Gunther _____ ounces
_____ pound(s) _____ ounce(s)

2. How much did each bear's lightest fish weigh in ounces?

Gus = _____   **Garth** = _____   **Gary** = _____   **Gunther** = _____

3. Which bear won the contest? _____

> **Bonus Box:** Calculate the total weight of each bear's catch of fish.

Pour It On!

Shower your students with practice in measuring metric capacity and watch their knowledge overflow!

Purpose: To choose an appropriate unit of measure for metric capacity

Students will do the following:

- choose between milliliters and liters as the appropriate unit of measure

Materials for each student:

- copy of page 14
- pencil

Vocabulary to review:

- milliliters (ml)
- liters (l)

Extension activities to use after the reproducible:

- Keep this game, called Stick With Metrics!, on file to provide students with more practice using milliliters and liters. Cut from magazines and grocery store ads pictures of items that are measured in either milliliters or liters. (Be sure the actual measurements aren't visible on the pictures.) Laminate them; then attach a small piece of Velcro® to the back of each. Next, open a file folder. Label one side "Milliliters" and the other side "Liters." Attach corresponding pieces of Velcro to each side. Have pairs of students choose a picture and decide if that item should be measured in milliliters or liters. Tell them to attach the card to the appropriate side. On the back of the folder, write which items belong in each category. Students check their answers by flipping over the folder. They're sure to stick with metrics!

- Pour on practice in estimating and measuring with this hands-on activity. Round up containers in interesting shapes and varied sizes. Fill them with water. Have small groups of students examine each and predict how many milliliters or liters of water it contains. Then show students how to use a graduated cylinder or metric measuring cup to carefully measure the water to the nearest milliliter or liter. For added interest, use colored water or colored sand for the measurements. Let the learning flow!

Pour It On!

Millie's Metric Market is bustling with busy shoppers. But sometimes Millie's customers aren't sure what size of a particular item they should buy. Help them by reading the problems below. Write the correct answer in the blank on each item's label.

1. Scout Troop #77 is hosting a spaghetti dinner for all of the scouts and their families. Should they buy 500 ml or 50 l of spaghetti sauce?

2. Sandy Tanner is going to the beach. She needs to buy sunscreen. Should she purchase 200 ml or 2 l of sunscreen?

3. Thirsty Theo just got a can of soda. Does the can hold 450 ml or 450 l of soda?

4. Mrs. Beetle is buying juice for a party in her fifth-grade classroom. Should she buy 10 ml or 10 l of juice?

5. Tom Mato is stocking up on single-serving ketchup packets for the school cafeteria. Does each packet hold 35 ml or 3 l of ketchup?

6. Fido is painting his doghouse. Should he purchase 800 ml or 8 l of paint?

Bonus Box: Based on your answers above, add the total number of liters and milliliters that Millie will sell at her store today.

©2001 The Education Center, Inc. • *Math Skills Workout* • TEC3229 • Key p. 167

The Capacity Game

Use this game to help your students practice their skills at converting customary units of capacity.

Purpose: To convert customary units of capacity

Students will do the following:

- play a game on converting customary units of capacity

Materials for each student:

- copy of page 16
- pencil
- game piece for each player
- die
- copy of the answer key (see page 167)

Vocabulary to review:

- cup
- pint
- quart
- half gallon
- gallon

It takes 16 of you to equal me!

Show-off!

Extension activities to use after the reproducible:

- To continue practicing converting customary units of capacity, create a matching game with problems similar to those used in the game on page 16. Gather twenty 5" x 8" index cards. On each of ten cards, write a different customary unit of capacity. Then, on each of the remaining ten cards, write a different unit of capacity that is equivalent to one of the first ten cards. For example, if a card from the first stack reads "12 pints," its matching card in the other pile could read "6 quarts." Shuffle both piles of cards together; then tape each card facedown to the chalkboard. Divide the class into two teams. Have Team 1 send a student to the board to try to flip over two matching cards. If a match is made, the team gets to keep the pair. If not, the cards are returned facedown on the board. Next, have Team 2 send a student to the board to repeat the process. Continue until all ten matches are made. The team with the most matches is the winner!

- Help your students practice using their capacity-estimating skills with the following activity. Display an oversized jar filled with rice. Have each student predict how many cups, pints, quarts, or gallons of rice are contained in the jar. Record each student's estimation on the board. Then have a student volunteer use a measuring cup to scoop out and measure the exact amount of rice. Treat the students with the closest estimates to a special treat.

The Capacity Game

Number of players: 3–4

Materials: gameboard, game piece for each player, die

Directions: Place the game pieces on the Start space. Select a player to sit out of the game to be the scorekeeper and the answer checker (using the answer key provided by your teacher). The first player rolls the die and then moves his game piece that number of spaces. Next, the player must correctly convert the unit of capacity shown on the space to the new unit of capacity. If the player is correct, he earns 1 point. If he is incorrect, the player earns no points. Continue this process with each player. Once each player reaches the Finish square of the game, the player with the most points wins. Play again to allow the scorekeeper to play the game.

START

1. 1 gallon = _____ quarts

2. $\frac{3}{4}$ quart = _____ cups

3. **GO BACK 2 SPACES**
   $\frac{1}{2}$ gallon = _____ pints

4. $3\frac{1}{2}$ pints = _____ cups

5. 20 cups = _____ quarts

Move Ahead 2 Spaces

6. 6 pints = _____ quarts

7. 8 cups = _____ pints

8. $\frac{1}{4}$ gallon = _____ cups

Lose a Turn

9. 8 quarts = _____ gallons

10. 10 pints = _____ quarts

11. 2 gallons = _____ pints

12. 5 pints = _____ cups

GO BACK 2 SPACES

13. 3 quarts = _____ pints

14. $\frac{3}{4}$ gallon = _____ pints

15. 16 pints = _____ quarts

Extra Turn

16. 32 cups = _____ gallons

2 pints = 1 quart   2 quarts = $\frac{1}{2}$ gallon   4 quarts = 1 gallon

2 cups = 1 pint

17. 16 pints = _____ gallons

18. 9 quarts = _____ cups

19. 12 quarts = _____ gallons

20. 20 quarts = _____ gallons

FINISH

Spinning Over Celsius

Send your students spinning with this Celsius activity!

Purpose: To correctly calculate the increase or decrease of Celsius temperature

Students will do the following:

- calculate the increase and decrease of Celsius temperatures
- illustrate temperatures on Celsius thermometer models
- correctly read a Celsius thermometer

Materials for each student:

- copy of page 18
- pencil
- paper clip
- red marker

Vocabulary to review:

- Celsius
- degree
- temperature
- increase and decrease

COME ON DOWN!

Extension activities to use after the reproducible:

- Hold a Celsius temperature-predicting contest! On a Friday afternoon, write the following headings horizontally across the top of a sheet of chart paper: Monday, Tuesday, Wednesday, Thursday, and Friday. Then have each student come up and write his predicted high Celsius temperature for each day of the upcoming week. Make sure the student writes his name beside his prediction. Each day of the following week, have students watch the weather section of the evening news or check the newspaper for the day's high temperature. Then, the next day, reward each student who came within five degrees of the high temperature with a special treat. Continue this process for each day on the chart.

- The following Celsius matching game is perfect in a math center. Duplicate page 18; then cut out each Celsius thermometer pattern. Paste each pattern onto a separate index card. Use a red marker to shade in a different degree of temperature on each thermometer pattern. Next, write the numerical value of each temperature on a separate index card. Have students play the game in pairs. Instruct the pair to place all the cards facedown on a table. Instruct one student to flip over two cards at a time to find a matching thermometer and written temperature. If the student finds a match, he gets to keep the cards and try again. If a match is not made, the cards are returned to their original positions facedown on the table and the other student takes a turn. The game is played until all the matches are made. The student with the most matches is the winner.

Spinning Over Celsius

Directions: Below each thermometer you will find a starting Celsius temperature. For each starting Celsius temperature, use the spinner below to create a temperature increase or decrease. If your spin lands on an "Add" space, circle "Increase" underneath the starting Celsius temperature. If your spin lands on a "Subtract" space, circle "Decrease" underneath the starting Celsius temperature. Then write the number of degrees to be added or subtracted in the blank. Next, calculate the temperature increase or decrease to find the final temperature. Finally, use a red marker to color in each Celsius thermometer to match the final temperature.

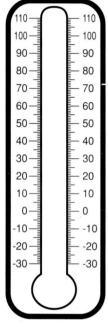 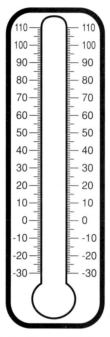 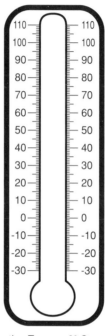 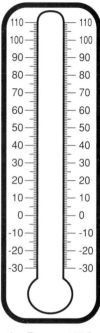

1. Starting Temp. = 27° C

Temp. Increase/Decrease = _____

Final Temp. = _____

2. Starting Temp. = 40° C

Temp. Increase/Decrease = _____

Final Temp. = _____

3. Starting Temp. = 2° C

Temp. Increase/Decrease = _____

Final Temp. = _____

4. Starting Temp. = 18° C

Temp. Increase/Decrease = _____

Final Temp. = _____

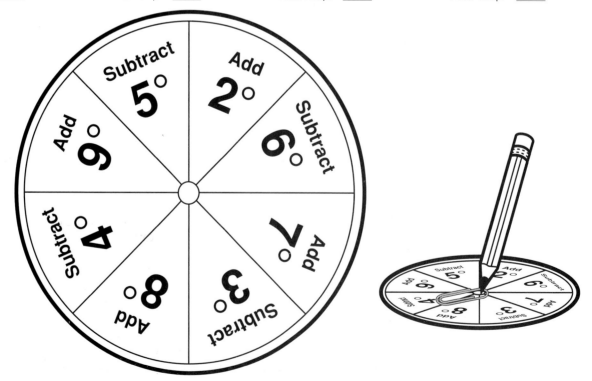

Fun With Fahrenheit

Warm students up to Fahrenheit with this fun activity!

Purpose: To correctly measure temperature in degrees Fahrenheit

Students will do the following:
- choose reasonable Fahrenheit temperatures for given situations
- locate temperatures on a Fahrenheit thermometer

Materials for each student:
- copy of page 20
- pencil

Vocabulary to review:
- Fahrenheit
- reasonable
- degree

Whew!

Extension activities to use after the reproducible:
- Every week has its highs and lows. Have your students track the high and low temperatures for each day of a given week. To begin, make ten copies of the Fahrenheit thermometer pattern on page 164. Each day have a student or group of students measure the outside temperature at the beginning of the day and at the end of the day. Each time the temperature is measured, have the student label one of the Fahrenheit thermometer patterns with the date and time. Then have him use a red marker to color in the temperature measured. Display the thermometer patterns for each day on a bulletin board titled "Our Highs and Lows."

- Combine science and math with this great idea! At the beginning of the day, present to your students four paper cups, each filled with one of the following items: sand, cotton balls, stones/gravel, and water. Next, have a student volunteer place one Fahrenheit thermometer into each cup. Then have another student place the four cups outside in a sunny spot or in a sunny windowsill. Every 30 minutes, have a student check the four cups and record the temperature shown on each of the four thermometers. Later in the day, discuss with your students the data collected. Have your students hypothesize why some thermometers had higher temperatures than others.

Fun With Fahrenheit

Complete the activity below to solve the riddle at the bottom of the page.

Directions: In each numbered blank below, write the letter of the most appropriate temperature labeled on the Fahrenheit thermometer. To solve the riddle at the bottom of the page, write each letter in the appropriate numbered blank.

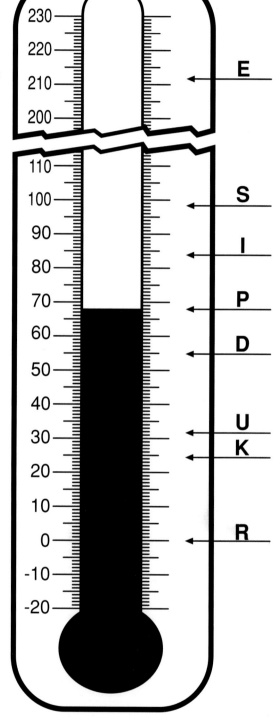

_____ 1. A warm day

_____ 2. Water boils

_____ 3. Inside a freezer

_____ 4. Water freezes

_____ 5. Room temperature

_____ 6. Winter jacket weather

_____ 7. Normal body temperature

_____ 8. Sweater weather

Riddle:

What does your teacher see each time you greet her at the start of the day?

A $\dfrac{}{7}$ $\dfrac{}{4}$ $\dfrac{}{5}$ $\dfrac{}{2}$ $\dfrac{}{3}$ $\dfrac{}{6}$ $\dfrac{}{1}$ $\dfrac{}{8}$

Bonus Box: On the back of this sheet, write a short story about the activities you might do on a day that has a temperature of 85°F.

Time to Solve a Mystery

Demystify calculating elapsed time for your students with this great activity!

Purpose: To calculate elapsed time

Students will do the following:

- interpret time clues in order to calculate elapsed time
- compare times calculated in order to identify the latest time
- solve problems

Materials for each student:

- copy of page 22
- pencil

Vocabulary to review:

- elapsed time

Extension activities to use after the reproducible:

- Help your students get a handle on how much time they spend on different activities throughout the day with the following activity. Have each student record a schedule of her activities from the time she wakes up to the time she goes to bed. On the next day, direct each student to determine the amount of time she spent on each activity. Next, have her trade schedules with another student, check the other student's answers for accuracy, and ask him four questions about his schedule. For example: How much time passes between the starting and ending times of the first and second activities? In which activity were you participating when it was 1 hour and 30 minutes after lunch?

- Create a great game to be used as a warm-up to or a review of elapsed time! Gather 14 index cards (or half the number of students in your class). Label each of seven cards with a different time. Then label each of the remaining seven cards with a time that is equal to but reads differently than each of the previously labeled cards. For example, if one of the first cards reads 5:45 P.M., then the matching card could read 15 minutes before 6:00 P.M. To play the game, divide your students into 14 pairs. Give each pair one card. Call on one pair to read the time written on its card. Instruct the pair that has the matching time to stand up and read its time. Continue this process until all the matches have been made.

Time to Solve a Mystery

At Molly Manner's birthday party, the special slice of birthday cake that Molly had saved was discovered missing shortly after the last guest left. Although each party guest denies taking the cake, Molly believes the last guest to leave the party was the "cakenapper"! To solve the mystery and find out that person's name, use the clues below. Read all the clues carefully. Then write in the blank beside each name the actual time that guest left the party.

Yikes! Someone stole my cake!

Clues:

_____ 1. Mabel McGraw left 20 minutes before Mandy Mercer.

_____ 2. Melvin Mackey left 40 minutes before Mike Mancini.

_____ 3. Missy Morton left 30 minutes after Mandy Mercer.

_____ 4. Marco Marino left 25 minutes before Marvin Merriweather.

_____ 5. Max Miffleburg left 20 minutes before Marcie Minster.

_____ 6. Mike Mancini left 20 minutes before 7:00 P.M.

_____ 7. Mandy Mercer left 55 minutes after Melvin Mackey.

_____ 8. Marvin Merriweather left 45 minutes after Marcie Minster.

_____ 9. Maggie Magoo left 35 minutes after Mike Mancini.

_____ 10. Marcie Minster left 30 minutes after Melvin Mackey.

Molly believes the cakenapper is _____.

Bonus Box: Which party guest left 2 hours and 25 minutes before 9:05 P.M.?

A Monster of a Marathon!

Help your students run toward success in calculating elapsed time!

Purpose: To calculate elapsed time

Students will do the following:

- calculate elapsed time from A.M. to P.M.
- order amounts of time from fastest to slowest

Materials for each student:

- copy of page 24
- pencil

Vocabulary to review:

- elapsed time
- A.M. and P.M.
- fastest time
- slowest time

I hope I make it in under four hours!

Extension activities to use after the reproducible:

- Obtain a copy of a commuter or national train schedule for a station near you. Divide your students into pairs. Give each pair a copy of the train schedule. Instruct each pair to develop five to ten questions that can be answered by reading and interpreting the schedule and calculating elapsed time. For example: Train 1551 leaves New Carrollton at 4:43 P.M. It arrives in Philadelphia at 6:35 P.M. How long is this train ride? Have each pair switch its list of questions with another pair. Instruct each pair to answer the questions using the schedule; then have each pair return the list of answered questions to the owners to be checked for accuracy.

- Get one index card for each student. On half of the cards, write a period of time, such as "10:45 A.M. to 1:35 P.M." On the other half of the cards, record the elapsed time to match each of the time-period cards. Next, shuffle the cards, and distribute one card to each student. Direct each student with a time-period card to calculate the elapsed time. Then, at your signal, have each of those students find the classmate who has the matching elapsed-time card. After all the matches have been made, collect and reshuffle the cards, and play another round!

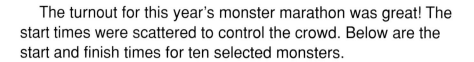

A Monster of a Marathon!

The turnout for this year's monster marathon was great! The start times were scattered to control the crowd. Below are the start and finish times for ten selected monsters.

Directions: Calculate the amount of time it took for each monster to finish the marathon. Record the amount of time for each monster in the Elapsed Time column. Then use the elapsed time for each monster to help you determine the finish place order. For example, the monster with the shortest amount of elapsed time would have the number 1 in his/her Finish Place box.

Monster	Start Time	Finish Time	Elapsed Time	Finish Place
1. **Marvin**	8:05 A.M.	12:12 P.M.		
2. **Maurice**	9:20 A.M.	12:55 P.M.		
3. **Marty**	9:33 A.M.	1:17 P.M.		
4. **Martha**	9:47 A.M.	1:45 P.M.		
5. **Marie**	10:10 A.M.	1:23 P.M.		
6. **Molly**	10:25 A.M.	1:15 P.M.		
7. **Margo**	11:12 A.M.	3:00 P.M.		
8. **Max**	11:30 A.M.	4:09 P.M.		
9. **Mandi**	11:41 A.M.	4:35 P.M.		
10. **Marcy**	11:56 A.M.	5:02 P.M.		

Bonus Box: Calculate the elapsed time between the start time of the first monster and the finish time of the last monster.

©2001 The Education Center, Inc. • *Math Skills Workout* • TEC3229 • Key p. 167

Fabulous Floor Plan Contest

Turn your students into designers with this floor plan activity.

Purpose: To design a floor plan in square units

Students will do the following:

- create a floor plan in square units according to specifications
- label each item correctly on the floor plan

Materials for each student:

- copy of page 26
- pencil
- markers, crayons (optional)
- grid paper (see page 163)

Vocabulary to review:

- floor plan
- square unit

This floor plan is great!

Extension activities to use after the reproducible:

- Combine writing and math with the following activity. Inform your students that they are up-and-coming new floor plan designers. Instruct each student to write a letter to a prospective client persuading her to select his floor plan for her new house. Inform the student to be sure to include a detailed description of the floor plan and a blueprint of the floor plan in square units.

- Have students create a blueprint for a new school playground. Give each student one copy of the grid paper on page 163. Encourage your students to be as creative and detailed as possible, including items such as a jungle gym area, basketball courts, a soccer field, a foursquare area, a seesaw area, a merry-go-round area, etc. Post each student's blueprint on a board for all to dream about and enjoy.

Fabulous Floor Plan Contest

Rocky owns the local roller rink and has decided to remodel. He's having a design contest to find the best floor plan. The winner will receive free skating for a lifetime.

Directions: Listed below are all the items that must be included in each submitted floor plan. On a separate sheet of grid paper, design a floor plan to enter into the contest. Be sure to include and label each item/area that Rocky has listed below.

Design Contest Requirements

- **Skating area** = 96 square units

- **2 locker areas** = 4 square units each

- **8 benches** = 6 square units each

- **Rental skate storage room** = 16 square units

- **Skate rental counter** = 6 square units

- **Snack bar** = 28 square units
  Inside snack bar:
  - **Kitchen counter** = 4 square units
  - **4 tables** = 1 square unit each

- **Game room** = 24 square units
  Inside game room:
  - **Pool table** = 6 square units
  - **Car racing game** = 2 square units
  - **Motorcycle racing game** = 2 square units
  - **Pinball machine** = 2 square units

- **DJ booth** = 9 square units

I can't wait to see these designs!

Bonus Box: Compare the areas of the skating area, snack bar, and game room. How much larger is the skating area than the snack bar? How much smaller is the game room than the snack bar?

Playing Around With Area

Make calculating area fun for your students with the following activity!

Purpose: To calculate the given area of an irregularly shaped polygon

Students will do the following:

- calculate the area of irregularly shaped polygons within a floor plan
- convert measurements using a scale

Materials for each student:

- copy of page 28
- pencil
- centimeter ruler

Vocabulary to review:

- area
- dimensions
- square centimeters
- square meters

one meter

Extension activities to use after the reproducible:

- Have each student find the area of a room at home, such as his bedroom, the kitchen, or the family room. Instruct the student to use a metric ruler, meterstick, or tape measure to measure the length and width of the selected room to the nearest centimeter. Then have him use the formula A = L x W to calculate the area of the room in square centimeters.

- Use this hands-on activity to help students practice their knowledge of area. Divide your students into small groups. Give each group a different-sized box. Instruct each group to calculate the total surface area of the outside of its box. Guide each group into understanding that it will need to calculate the area of each side and then add the areas of the sides together to get the total surface area of the box. Have the groups switch boxes to check each other's calculations.

Playing Around With Area

Today is the grand opening of the Kit E. Kat Community Center! Use the floor plan below to calculate the area of each room within the center.

Directions: The dimensions of each room in the floor plan are measured in centimeters. Use a centimeter ruler to help you calculate the area of each room in square centimeters. Record your answers in the chart below. *(Hint: Break apart each section into smaller parts. Calculate the area of each smaller section; then add them together to get the total area.)* Then convert each area measurement using the scale to give you a more real-life measurement for each room. *(Hint: On this floor plan, 1 square centimeter equals 10 square meters.)*

Scale: 1 square centimeter = 10 square meters

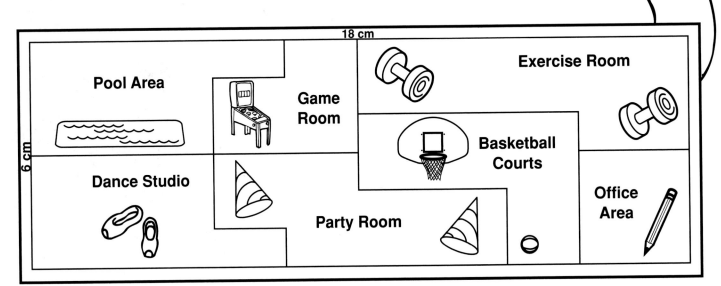

Kit E. Kat Community Center Rooms	Area in Square Centimeters	Real-Life Area in Square Meters
1. Pool Area		
2. Dance Studio		
3. Party Room		
4. Game Room		
5. Exercise Room		
6. Basketball Courts		
7. Office Area		

Bonus Box: What is the total area covered by the community center? Write your answer in square meters.

Something New at the Zoo

Show students that calculating area can be a "zoo-rific" task!

Purpose: To calculate area in metric units

Students will do the following:

- calculate area of rectangles using given dimensions
- construct a floor plan using a given set of dimensions

Materials for each student:

- copy of page 30
- pencil
- centimeter grid paper (see page 163)

Vocabulary to review:

- area
- dimensions
- square centimeters

CITY ZOO

Extension activities to use after the reproducible:

- Have students find shapes in the school to calculate the area of, such as a bulletin board, the blacktop, or the cafeteria floor. Have each student select an item or location to measure. Next, have him estimate the area and then use a meterstick or tape measure to measure and calculate the actual area. Post the results on a bulletin board titled "How Our School Measures Up."

- Combine art and math to help reinforce the concept of area with your students. Give each student one blank sheet of centimeter grid paper (see page 163). Direct each student to color the squares on her grid paper to create a picture of an object or figure, such as a tree, the sun, or an animal. After the student completes her picture, have her estimate its area. Then have the student count the actual number of squares to check the accuracy of her estimate. Have each student share her picture and calculation with the class.

Something New at the Zoo

Zeek the zookeeper has just determined the dimensions for the animal sites in the new African Safari section of the city zoo. He needs your help to create a blueprint or layout showing the location and size of each new animal site. Use the dimensions listed below to help you calculate the area of each site in square centimeters. Then use the area of each site and a sheet of centimeter grid paper to help you design a blueprint or layout of the African Safari section of the zoo. Be sure to clearly label each site with its name and total area in square centimeters.

Animal	Site Dimensions	Calculated Area in Square Centimeters
1. zebras	4 cm x 7 cm	
2. elephants	5 cm x 9 cm	
3. hyenas	5 cm x 5 cm	
4. monkeys	3 cm x 9 cm	
5. birds	3 cm x 6 cm	
6. lions	3 cm x 5 cm	
7. antelope	2 cm x 11 cm	
8. cheetahs	4 cm x 8 cm	
9. crocodiles	3 cm x 4 cm	
10. rhinos	4 cm x 5 cm	

Bonus Box: List the animal sites in order from the largest area to the smallest area. Then write a math word problem using this information.

Plowing Through Perimeter

Use this activity to plant the concept of perimeter in the minds of your students.

Purpose: To determine all possible metric dimensions for shapes with specific perimeters

Students will do the following:
- construct squares and rectangles with specific perimeters
- find perimeter in metric units

Materials for each student:
- copy of page 32
- pencil

Vocabulary to review:
- dimensions
- perimeter

Extension activities to use after the reproducible:

- Tell your students that you've decided the school needs a new fence around the playground. Explain that the class has to help the school determine how much fence will be needed and how much it will cost. Have your students use a tape measure to measure the perimeter of your playground. To get a realistic idea of fence prices, call a local fencing company to get a quoted price for chain-link fencing per foot or yard. *(You'll need to convert feet/yards to meters and adjust the dollar amount.)* Next, have your students calculate the cost of the fence based on the perimeter of the playground and the quoted price for the fence.

- Draw on a sheet of paper a square, a rectangle, and an equilateral triangle. Then duplicate the page for each student. Challenge each student to use what she knows about perimeter to determine alternate methods of calculating perimeter besides adding together the length of all the shape's sides. Have the student think about how multiplication can be integrated into a formula.

32 Name _____

Plowing Through Perimeter

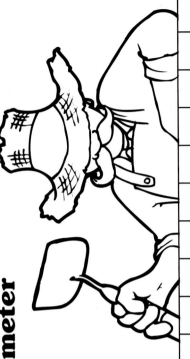

Directions: You've been hired as the head gardener at the botanical gardens. Your first job is to design 6 flower beds. Each bed has to be a square or a rectangle, and each bed has to have a perimeter of 24 meters. The only catch is that no 2 beds can be exactly the same. On the grid below, draw and label the 6 different ways of creating a flower bed with a perimeter of 24 meters.

Each ☐ **= 1 square meter.**

Bonus Box: How many different square or rectangular flower beds could you create with a perimeter of 30 meters each?

Perimeter Gone Nutty

Use this activity and your students will go nuts over perimeter!

Purpose: To measure perimeter in customary units

Students will do the following:
- measure perimeter of irregularly shaped polygons
- measure in inches and half inches

Materials for each student:
- copy of page 34
- pencil
- ruler

Vocabulary to review:
- perimeter
- dimensions

Extension activities to use after the reproducible:
- Divide your students into small groups. Cut a different irregularly shaped polygon from tagboard for each group. Give each group three to five minutes to measure and record on a sheet of paper the perimeter of its polygon. Then have each group switch polygons with another group. Continue this process until all groups have measured and recorded the perimeter for each polygon. Then have each group read aloud the perimeter it recorded for each polygon. Write each group's responses on the board. Have the groups compare the data. Remeasure any polygons where there may be discrepancies in the students' data.

- Provide each student with a ruler. Have each student find three items in, on, or around his desk, such as a textbook, novel, notebook, pencil case, or desktop. Then instruct each student to measure and calculate the perimeter of each item. Have each student read aloud his three perimeters. Award a special treat to the student who has the object with the smallest perimeter and the student who has the object with the largest perimeter.

Perimeter Gone Nutty

Selma Squirrel found a chocolate-covered peanut candy bar and decided to bring it back to the nest to share with her brothers and sisters. When she unwrapped it, she found that it was cracked into the exact number of pieces that she needed. She labeled each piece with a sibling's name.

Directions: Use a ruler to measure the sides of each piece of chocolate to the nearest inch or half inch, whichever is closer. To calculate the perimeter of each piece of chocolate, add all the sides together. Write the total perimeter for each piece of chocolate in the blank beside each squirrel's name.

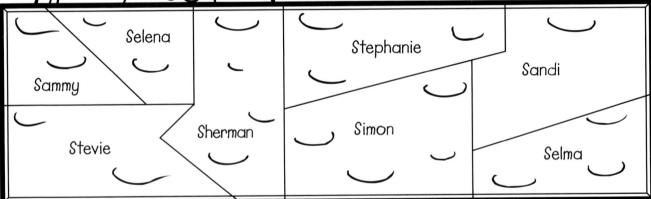

1. Sammy   P = _____

2. Stevie   P = _____

3. Selena   P = _____

4. Stephanie   P = _____

5. Sherman   P = _____

6. Simon   P = _____

7. Sandi   P = _____

8. Selma   P = _____

Bonus Box: Calculate the average perimeter of the pieces of chocolate above.

Remodeling Dilemma

This fun setting should definitely keep your students' attention.

Purpose: To calculate perimeter and area in customary units

Students will do the following:

- use a diagram to solve word problems
- calculate perimeter or area in customary units

Materials for each student:

- copy of page 36
- pencil

Vocabulary to review:

- area
- perimeter

Hmmm... area or perimeter?

Extension activities to use after the reproducible:

- Use the following math journal prompts to help your students better understand perimeter and area:

    Prompt #1: Jamie needs to retile the kitchen floor. He's not sure how many 1 ft. x 1 ft. tiles to buy. He does know that the floor measures 15 ft. x 18 ft. What can Jamie do to figure out how many tiles to buy to cover the kitchen floor? Explain your answer in writing.

    Prompt #2: Sarah wants to put a wooden border in front of the hedges that surround her backyard. She's not sure how much wood to buy. She does know that her backyard measures 25 yds. x 20 yds. Help Sarah figure out how much wood to buy and explain your solution in writing.

- Give each student two index cards. Instruct each student to make up one area word problem and one perimeter word problem. Direct the student to write each problem on a separate card. Once each student has written both word problems, have him trade cards with another student. Instruct each student to solve the two new word problems he receives. Continue having students trade cards until each student has the opportunity to solve two or three sets of cards. If desired, collect all the cards and place them in a math center for students to solve during their free time.

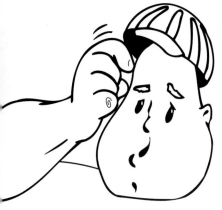

Remodeling Dilemma

Al's Amusement Center is temporarily closed due to remodeling. The remodeling crew is hard at work making improvements, but the crew is getting stumped over when to calculate area or perimeter.

Directions: Read each problem below. Then circle area or perimeter below each problem to show which one the crew needs to calculate to solve the problem. Next, use the labeled floor plan to help you solve each problem. Write each answer in the solution blank provided.

	40 ft.	25 ft.	55 ft.	30 ft.	
25 ft.	In-line Skating	Arcade	Bumper Cars	Snack Bar	25 ft.
30 ft.	Go-Carts	Miniature Golf		Batting Cage	30 ft.
	40 ft.	80 ft.		30 ft.	

1. The go-cart track needs a new bumper pad to line all 4 walls. How many feet of bumper padding should be ordered?

   Area   **Perimeter**   Solution: _____

2. The in-line skating rink floor is being replaced with new 1 ft. x 1 ft. tiles. How many tiles will be needed to cover the rink?

   Area   **Perimeter**   Solution: _____

3. The crew is adding carpet to the arcade area. What is the total amount of carpet needed?

   Area   **Perimeter**   Solution: _____

4. The crew is placing a new fence around the miniature golf course. How much fencing should be bought in order to surround the entire course?

   Area   **Perimeter**   Solution: _____

5. There will be lights strung around all sides of the batting cage area. How much lighting will be needed to outline the batting cages?

   Area   **Perimeter**   Solution: _____

6. The entire floor used for the bumper cars is being cleaned. The crew has 5 bottles of cleaner. Each bottle will cover 200 square feet. Is there enough cleaner? Why or why not?

   Area   **Perimeter**   Solution: _____

Bonus Box: The crew is putting in a climbing wall! It will be 50 feet high and 30 feet wide. Each 10 ft. x 10 ft. section of the wall costs $200.00 to install. How much will it cost to install the entire wall?

Measurement Mania

Make measurement review fun and games with this activity.

Purpose: To review customary measurement and elapsed time

Students will do the following:

- solve problems involving customary units of measurement
- calculate elapsed time

Materials for each student:

- copy of page 38
- pencil
- ruler

Vocabulary to review:

- customary unit
- linear
- mass
- capacity
- area
- perimeter
- temperature
- elapsed time

Extension activities to use after the reproducible:

- Write the following headings on the board: inches, feet, yards, miles, ounces, cups, pints, quarts, gallons, and Fahrenheit. Have each student get out five sheets of notebook paper and a pencil. Instruct the student to label the top of each sheet of paper (both front and back) with a different heading listed on the board. Then, at your signal, give your students ten minutes to list as many items as possible that can be measured in each particular unit of measurement. Afterward have students share their responses. Award the student(s) with the most items listed in each category a special prize.

- Divide your students into research teams to investigate where customary units of measurement originated and which countries still use customary units of measurement.

Name _____

38

Measurement Mania

Ladies and gentlemen, welcome to Measurement Mania! This is the place where contestants test their skills in customary measurement. Test your knowledge of customary measurement by solving each problem below.

Linear

1. Measure this candy to the nearest half inch.

Answer: _____

2. Measure this paper clip to the nearest half inch.

Answer: _____

3. Measure the width of your desk to the nearest inch.

Answer: _____

Area/Perimeter

4. Calculate the area of this rectangle.

16 ft.

8 ft.

Answer: _____

5. Bobby's uncle wants to build a fence around his yard. If the yard is 30 ft. x 20 ft., how much fencing will he need?

Answer: _____

Mass

6. 48 ounces = _____ pounds

7. 2 pounds 7 ounces = _____ ounces

8. Would your math book be more likely to weigh 3 ounces or 3 pounds?

Answer: _____

Capacity

9. 22 cups = _____ pints

10. 36 quarts = _____ gallons

11. 5 gallons = _____ cups

Reasonable Temperatures

12. Swimming   55°F   or   85°F

13. Sledding   32°F   or   55°F

14. Going on a picnic 92°F   or   78°F

Elapsed Time

15. It is 1 hour and 40 minutes after 8:15 A.M. What time is it?

Answer: _____

16. It is 55 minutes before 7:20 P.M. What time is it?

Answer: _____

17. Kevin arrived at the beach at 9:45 A.M. He left at 3:20 P.M. How long was Kevin at the beach?

Answer: _____

Metrics at the Movies

Give your students the ticket to a successful review of metric measurement.

Purpose: To review metric measurement

Students will do the following:
- solve problems using metric units of measurement

Materials for each student:
- copy of page 40
- pencil
- metric ruler

Vocabulary to review:
- linear measurement
- Celsius
- perimeter
- area
- mass
- capacity
- elapsed time

Extension activities to use after the reproducible:
- Have your students review metric measurement with the following game. Split metrics into categories: Linear Measurement, Temperature, Perimeter, Area, Mass, Capacity, and Time. For each category, provide three original word problems (or problems from the activities in this book). Write each word problem on one side of a 5" x 8" index card and write each category on the board. Tape each card facedown in a column under its category. Use a marker to label the back of each card with the following point scale: the first card = 5, the second card = 10, and the third card = 25. To play, divide the class into three groups. Have each group take turns selecting a category and problem. Group members have one minute to come up with the answer. If the group is incorrect, no points are awarded. Continue play until all the cards are answered.

- Have students brainstorm objects in the classroom/school that could be measured in meters, centimeters, millimeters, Celsius, milliliters, liters, milligrams, grams, and kilograms. Then have each student actually measure two of the objects listed under each of her categories.

Metrics at the Movies

Test your knowledge of metric measurement by answering each problem below.

1. Measure this piece of licorice to the nearest centimeter.

   Answer: _____

2. Patty always wears a sweater to the movies. Is the temperature in the theater probably closer to 15°C or 60°C?

   Answer: _____

3. Is a bag of popcorn more likely to weigh 50 g or 50 kg?

   Answer: _____

4. Will a large soda hold 250 ml, 5 l, or 1 l?

   Answer: _____

5. Before the new carpeting is put down in the theater, a tacking strip must be placed around the perimeter of the lobby floor. The floor measures 120 m x 60 m. What is the total length of tacking strip that will be needed?

   Answer: _____

6. A new movie poster needs to be hung up. It measures 90 cm x 50 cm. How much wall space will it cover?

   Answer: _____

7. The movie *Outer Space Adventure* begins at 7:15 P.M. and is over at 8:52 P.M. What is the length of this film?

   Answer: _____

8. List 3 real-life examples of ways people use metric measurement.

   1. _____

   2. _____

   3. _____

Under Construction

Build your students' knowledge of regular polygons
with this constructive geometry lesson!

Purpose: To identify regular polygons

Students will do the following:

- Identify regular polygons
- Color-code regular polygons hidden in a picture

Materials for each student:

- copy of page 42
- pencil
- crayon in each of the following colors: yellow, green, blue, orange, red, purple

Vocabulary to review:

- regular polygon
- triangle, square, pentagon, hexagon, octagon, decagon

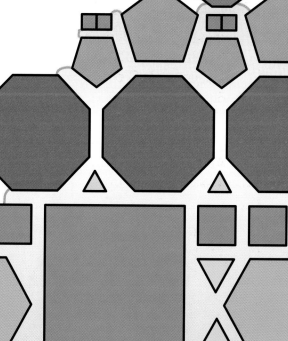

Extension activities to use after the reproducible:

- Use the following cooperative group activity to further extend your students' experiences with regular polygons. Divide your students into groups of four. Give each group ten 12-inch lengths of string. Next, call out the name of a regular polygon. Instruct each group to use its lengths of string to create the specified polygon. Inform your students that each side of the polygon consists of one 12-inch length of string. For example, three strings will build a triangle while six strings will build a hexagon.

- Use this quick and fun art activity to reinforce the concept of regular polygons. Give each student an old magazine and instruct her to find a real-life example of a triangle, a square, a pentagon, a hexagon, an octagon, or a decagon. Have her cut out each example and glue it onto the center of a sheet of drawing paper. Underneath each picture have her complete the following sentence: "A(n) _____ is an example of a(n) _____." Collect the shapes and bind them into a class book titled "Perfect Polygons!"

42

Under Construction

Harry Hexagon is building a wall using all types of polygons. He's really behind and needs your help. Harry needs to color all the regular polygons using the color code at the right. Help Harry locate and color each regular polygon in the wall below. Remember that a *regular polygon* is a polygon with all sides the same length and all angles the same measure.

Regular Polygons		
triangle	=	**yellow**
square	=	**green**
pentagon	=	**blue**
hexagon	=	**orange**
octagon	=	**red**
decagon	=	**purple**

Pricey Polygon Pictures

Have your students turn geometry into works of art
with this activity on polygons!

Purpose: To identify polygons

Students will do the following:

- design models of regular polygons on dot grids
- calculate the worth of a polygon picture using a key

Materials for each student:

- copy of page 44
- pencil
- pattern blocks or pattern block stencils
- crayons

Vocabulary to review:

- pattern blocks
- polygons
- worth

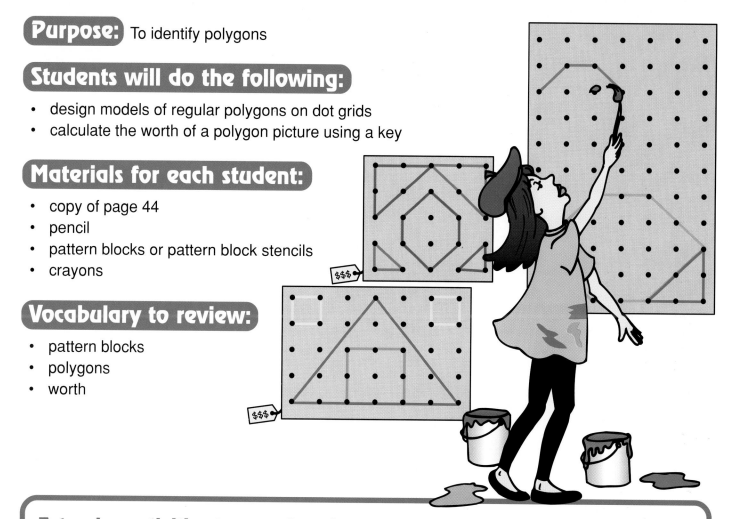

Extension activities to use after the reproducible:

- Use the following activity to reinforce the concepts presented on page 44. Provide each student with a set of pattern block stencils, drawing paper, and crayons. Instruct the student to use the stencils and a pencil to create a new design. Instruct the student to include every polygon shape at least once in her design. After a student completes her design, instruct her to create a bar graph or pictograph displaying the number of each shape used in the design. Then have the student write at least two sentences interpreting the graph, such as "I used three more hexagons than trapezoids. The shape I used the most was a triangle." Collect the assignments and display them on a bulletin board titled "Perfect Polygon Pictures!"

- Make vocabulary fun when you create a polygon picture dictionary! Have each student write each of the following terms at the top of a separate sheet of paper: *square, triangle, trapezoid, parallelogram, hexagon, polygon,* and *quadrilateral.* Then instruct the student to complete each page by drawing an example of the polygon underneath the appropriate term written on each sheet of paper. Then have the student look through old magazines for photograph examples of each polygon. Have the student cut out the magazine photo example and paste it underneath the appropriate drawing on the sheet of paper. Finally, have the student write a definition for each polygon underneath each photo example. Have the student stack the completed sheets and then staple them along the left-hand side to create his polygon picture dictionary booklet.

Pricey Polygon Pictures

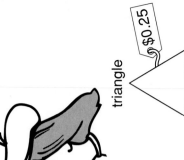

Teresa Trapezoid bases the cost of her drawings on the number of each kind of pattern block used. For example, a work of art that includes 6 hexagons, 3 trapezoids, 5 parallelograms, 10 squares, and 8 triangles would cost $25.75. This price is based on the key below.

hexagon
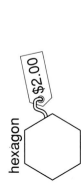
$2.00

trapezoid

$1.00

parallelogram

$0.75

square
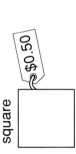
$0.50

triangle

$0.25

Try your hand at creating a pricey piece of art in the frame below! Your picture must meet the following requirements:

• total value is no more than $35.00
• includes at least 8 hexagons, 5 trapezoids, 4 parallelograms, 8 squares, 12 triangles
• has a title or name

My work of art is worth $ _____. On the back of this sheet, explain in writing how you arrived at this price.

©2001 The Education Center, Inc. • *Math Skills Workout* • TEC3229 • Key p. 168

Note to the teacher: Give each student the materials listed on page 43. Instruct each student to use a pencil to create the design described above by tracing the pattern blocks or stencils in the box above.

Is a Square Just a Square?

Help your students get squared away with this lesson on quadrilaterals.

Purpose: To identify and explain differences and similarities between five types of quadrilaterals

Students will do the following:

- classify different types of quadrilaterals
- identify and define different types of quadrilaterals
- sort quadrilaterals by definition
- write to explain differences and similarities

Materials for each student:

- copy of page 46
- pencil

Vocabulary to review:

- quadrilateral
- square, rectangle, parallelogram, rhombus, trapezoid
- parallel lines
- congruent
- similarities, differences

Extension activities to use after the reproducible:

- Help your students identify the attributes of various quadrilaterals with this class game. Cut out five construction paper patterns of each of the following quadrilaterals: square, rectangle, parallelogram, rhombus, trapezoid. Place the cutouts in a paper bag. Shake the bag. Then have a student volunteer turn his back to the class and select one shape from the bag without revealing it to the class. Direct him to list three clues to the shape's identity on the board. Have the student call on a classmate to read the clues from the board and identify the shape. If the classmate is correct, have her select the next shape from the bag and list three clues to its identity. If she is incorrect, have the original student volunteer call on another classmate to answer.

- After completing page 46, have each student create a riddle for each quadrilateral. Then divide your students into pairs. Instruct one member of each pair to read each riddle to his partner. Have the pair record how many of the riddles were answered correctly. Then have each pair repeat the process with the other partner reading his riddles. Treat the pair with the most correctly answered riddles to a special prize.

Is a Square Just a Square?

Mr. Blockhead, a toy maker, has been hired to make a set of quadrilateral blocks. In planning the set, he has become very confused by directions left by his boss. For example, the directions say a square is a rectangle, but a rectangle is not a square. Help Mr. Blockhead figure out the directions by completing the tasks below.

Task #1: Carefully read each definition in the box below. Then write inside each illustrated quadrilateral the number of each definition that describes that quadrilateral. *Hint: Some may have more than 1 definition.*

Quadrilaterals

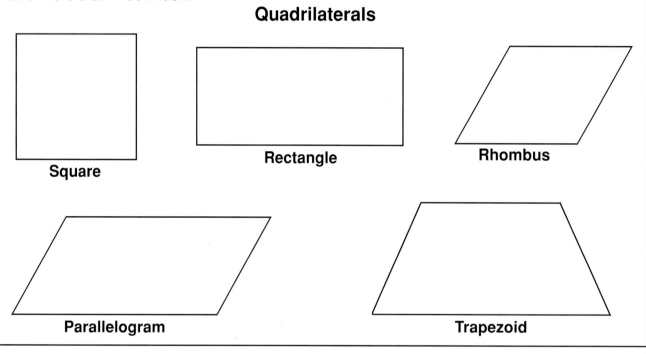

Definitions

1. a 4-sided figure in which each set of opposite sides is equal in length and parallel
2. a 4-sided figure with 4 congruent sides
3. a 4-sided figure with 4 90° angles
4. a 4-sided figure with 4 90° angles and 4 congruent sides
5. a 4-sided figure with only 1 set of parallel lines

Task #2: Mark each statement as true or false.
   a. A square is a kind of rectangle.
   b. A rectangle is a kind of square.
   c. A parallelogram is a kind of rhombus.
   d. A rhombus is a kind of parallelogram.
   e. A square is a kind of parallelogram.

Task #3: Think about the definitions of a square and a rectangle. Then, on the back of this page, write a brief paragraph explaining their similarities and differences.

©2001 The Education Center, Inc. • *Math Skills Workout* • TEC3229 • Key p. 169

It's All Related

Introduce your students to space figures and their related characteristics with the following lesson.

Purpose: To identify and explain the characteristics of space figures

Students will do the following:

- identify and count the number of edges, faces, and vertices of space figures
- explain the similarities of various space figures by comparing the number of edges, faces, and vertices of each space figure

Materials for each student:

- copy of page 48
- pencil

Vocabulary to review:

- faces
- vertices
- edges
- cube, rectangular prism, triangular prism, square pyramid, rectangular pyramid, triangular pyramid

Extension activities to use after the reproducible:

- Collect a variety of items that represent each space figure featured in the lesson—cube, rectangular prism, triangular prism, square pyramid, rectangular pyramid, triangular pyramid. As a class, sort the items into the appropriate space-figure categories. Next, divide your students into pairs. Give each pair one space-figure item from one of the categories. Then instruct the pair to describe the object using geometric terms. For example, an eraser may be described as a rectangular prism with 12 edges, six faces, and eight vertices. Encourage students to also include other descriptive information, such as color, size, weight, and texture. Collect the descriptions and read them aloud to the class. Have student volunteers try to guess which item is being described.

- Help further reinforce the names of space figures in a flash with the following activity. Give each student 12 large index cards, an old magazine, scissors, glue, and a rubber band. Instruct each student to peruse the magazine to find two examples of each space figure listed on page 48. Have the student cut out and glue a different picture to one side of each index card and then write the name of that space figure on the back of the card. Direct the student to use the rubber band to bind the cards together. During free time, have students use their flash cards alone or with a partner to practice identifying each geometric figure.

It's All Related

Max loves math! His teacher has told him that there is a special connection between the space figures in the chart below. Help Max find the special connection between each space figure by completing the chart and activities below.

Face — a flat surface of a space figure
Edge — a line segment formed where 2 faces of a space figure intersect
Vertex — a common endpoint of 2 rays forming an angle, 2 line segments forming sides of a polygon, or 2 line segments forming the edges of a space figure

1. Review the terms in the box above; then carefully count the number of edges, vertices, and faces of each space figure. Record your results in the table below.

Space Figure	Name	Number of Faces	Number of Vertices	Sum of Faces and Vertices	Number of Edges
	Cube				
	Rectangular Prism				
	Triangular Prism				
	Square Pyramid				
	Rectangular Pyramid				
	Triangular Pyramid				

2. Examine the data in the chart above. Compare the data recorded in the Sum of Faces and Vertices column with the data in the Number of Edges column for each space figure. What is the difference between the 2 numbers for each space figure?_____ Is the answer the same for each space figure? _____

3. Explain in a brief paragraph, on the back of this page, the special connection between each space figure in the chart above.

Bonus Box: A hexagonal prism is shown at the right. Count the number of faces, vertices, and edges. Does it also have the same special connection as the space figures shown above? ☐ Yes ☐ No

©2001 The Education Center, Inc. • *Math Skills Workout* • TEC3229 • Key p. 169

What's My Line?

Help your students become experts on lines, line segments, and rays with the following activity.

Purpose: To identify and construct a variety of lines, line segments, and rays

Students will do the following:

- identify and construct lines, line segments, and rays
- identify and construct parallel lines and perpendicular lines
- identify and use symbols for lines, line segments, rays, parallel lines, and perpendicular lines

Materials for each student:

- copy of page 50
- pencil
- ruler
- protractor

Vocabulary to review:

- line, line segment, ray
- parallel lines, intersecting lines, perpendicular lines

I have one endpoint and continue indefinitely in the opposite direction. What am I?

Hmmm.........

Extension activities to use after the reproducible:

- Have your students work in groups to find examples of lines, line segments, and rays in the classroom. Divide your students into six groups. Assign each group one of the following topics: lines, line segments, rays, parallel lines, intersecting lines, perpendicular lines. Give the groups approximately 15 minutes to explore the classroom and find examples of their assigned topics. After approximately 15 minutes, make six columns on the chalkboard. Assign each group a different column. Have one member of each group list the examples its group found for its topic. Have the class compare the information. Are there more examples of one type of line than another? Have your students explain why there may be more examples in one category than another.

- Supply each student with two sheets of drawing paper, a ruler, a protractor, and crayons or markers. Instruct each student to use the materials to create two different designs. Inform your students that the first design is to be made up of only one of the following: lines, line segments, or rays. Then tell each student that the second design is to consist of all three: lines, line segments, and rays. Have each student color both of his designs. Hang the designs around the classroom for all to enjoy.

What's My Line?

Complete the activity below to learn more about lines, line segments, and rays.

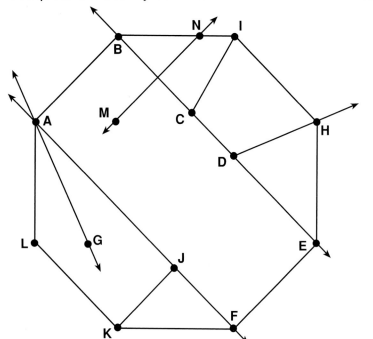

Word Box

Line—an endless set of points forming a straight path in opposite directions. The symbol for a line is ⟷.

Line segment—a part of a line with 2 definite endpoints. The symbol for a line segment is •——• .

Ray—a part of a line that has 1 endpoint and extends indefinitely from that point. The symbol for a ray is •——→.

Parallel lines—lines that always are the same distance apart and never cross. The symbol for parallel lines is **//**.

Intersecting lines—lines that meet or cross. The symbol for intersecting lines is ⨉ .

Perpendicular lines—2 lines that form right angles. The symbol for perpendicular lines is ⊥ .

Directions: Use the terms in the word box and the diagram above to help you complete 1–5 below.

1. List 2 lines that are parallel.
   _____ // _____

2. List 4 pairs of parallel line segments.
   _____ // _____; _____ // _____; _____ // _____; _____ // _____

3. List 2 intersecting lines.
   _____ ⨉ _____

4. Name 1 ray.

   _____

5. List 2 perpendicular lines.
   _____ ⊥ _____

6. Use a ruler and a protractor to help you draw a design in the box at the right that contains at least 1 example of each of the following:
   • line
   • line segment
   • ray
   • parallel lines
   • intersecting lines
   • perpendicular lines

©2001 The Education Center, Inc. • *Math Skills Workout* • TEC3229 • Key p. 169

Amazing Angles

Make your students proud as peacocks after completing this amazing lesson on angles!

Purpose: To measure angles

Students will do the following:

- measure angles using a protractor
- match solutions with words in a word box
- use answers to fill in missing words of a poem

Materials for each student:

- copy of page 52
- pencil
- protractor

Vocabulary to review:

- angle
- vertex
- protractor

Extension activities to use after the reproducible:

- Satisfy your students' hunger for both food and math with this tasty activity. Plan ahead of time to order one small pizza for each group of four students in your class. Draw four to eight (or more) angles of different degrees on an index card for each group. (Note: The angles in each set of cards must total 360° when added together.) Distribute the index cards, a protractor, and a pizza cutter to each group. Then instruct each group to cut its pizza into slices so that each angle on the index card is represented by a slice of pizza. Check each group's work. Then let them chow down and enjoy their hard work!

- Challenge your students with this activity on diagonals. Tell your students that a *diagonal* is a line segment that joins two vertices of a polygon but is not a side of the polygon. Some polygons have two diagonals and some have more than two. Sometimes diagonals will cross to form right angles. Make one copy of the polygons below for each student. Instruct each student to carefully look at each polygon. Then have him predict whether at least one set of diagonals within each polygon will cross to form right angles. Instruct the student to write "Yes" or "No" underneath each polygon. Then have the student draw in the diagonals using a pencil and a ruler. He can use a protractor or the corner of a sheet of paper to check for right angles. *(1. Yes; 2. No; 3. Yes; 4. No; 5. Yes; 6. No)*

1.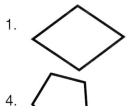

2.

3.

4.

5.

6.

Amazing Angles

Patrick Peacock is proud of all his feathers! He likes to spread them out for all to see. Listed below are different angles that can be found within his feathers. Each angle shares the same vertex. Use a protractor to measure each angle listed. Then find the degree of each angle in the answer box below and write the corresponding word in the appropriately numbered blank in the poem at the bottom of the page.

Angles

1. ∠ NAO
2. ∠ BAJ
3. ∠ EAR
4. ∠ DAG
5. ∠ GAL
6. ∠ BAP

7. ∠ IAP
8. ∠ CAR
9. ∠ KAT
10. ∠ MAQ
11. ∠ BAS
12. ∠ HAR

Answer Box

80°—heard
90°—doesn't
10°—haven't
150°—see
30°—feathered
50°—bird

70°—colors
130°—I'm
40°—everyone
100°—me
140°—rainbow
170°—be

Proud As a Peacock

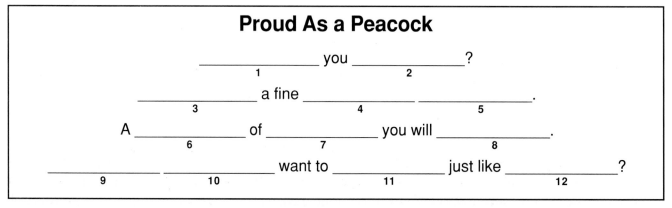

_____ you _____?
1   2

_____ a fine _____ _____.
3   4   5

A _____ of _____ you will _____.
6   7   8

_____ _____ want to _____ just like _____?
9   10   11   12

Going Ape Over Angles

Watch your students go bananas over this angle lesson that's packed with "a-peel"!

Purpose: To measure and identify acute, obtuse, and right angles

Students will do the following:

- identify acute, obtuse, and right angles
- use a protractor to measure angles
- write to explain the three types of angles

Materials for each student:

- copy of page 54
- pencil
- protractor

Vocabulary to review:

- acute angle
- obtuse angle
- right angle

Extension activities to use after the reproducible:

- Your study of angles will be right on time with the following activity! Give each student a copy of the clock face and hands on page 164, a pair of scissors, and one brad. Instruct each student to cut out the clock face and hands. Then have him attach the hands to the face using the brad. Next, call out different times of the day and have each student move the hands of his clock to represent the time called. Next, have the student use his protractor to measure the angle of the clock hands. Finally, have the student identify the type of angle formed by the clock's hands as acute, obtuse, or right.

- Help your students continue exploring angles using tangram pieces. Provide each student with a copy of the tangram pattern on page 165. Guide students in identifying the three polygons found in the tangram set. Then have each student measure the angles found in each polygon and identify them as acute, obtuse, or right.

Going Ape Over Angles

Albert the Ape loves to monkey around on his play equipment at the zoo! But now the zookeeper has given Albert an assignment: Measure each angle found in the equipment and label it as *acute*, *obtuse*, or *right*. See if you can help Albert by following the directions below.

Directions: Use a protractor to measure each lettered angle in the drawing. Then write the angle's measurement in the first blank and its name in the second blank. The first one has been done for you.

- An *acute* angle measures less than 90°.
- An *obtuse* angle measures more than 90°.
- A *right* angle measures exactly 90°.

	Measurement	Angle Name
A	105°	obtuse
B	_____	_____
C	_____	_____
D	_____	_____
E	_____	_____
F	_____	_____
G	_____	_____
H	_____	_____
I	_____	_____
J	_____	_____
K	_____	_____

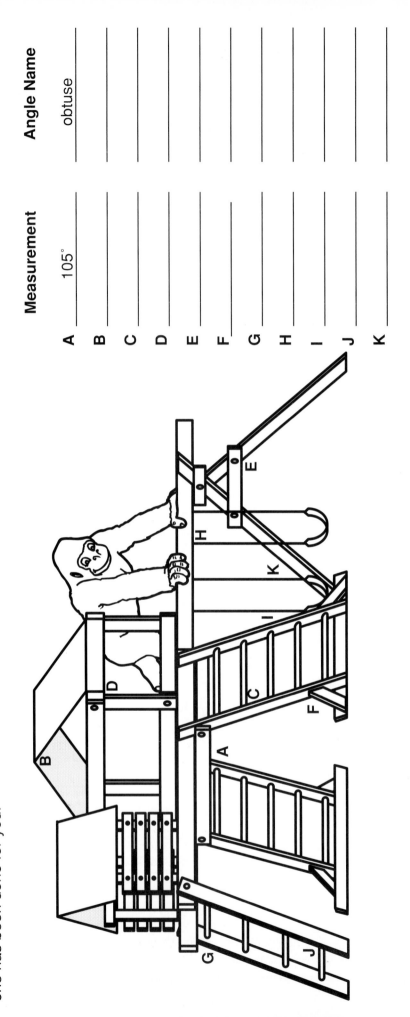

Bonus Box: Use the back of this page to write a short paragraph explaining the difference between an *acute* and an *obtuse* angle. Use illustrations to support your answer.

Similar Figures to the Rescue!

Make your students feel super knowledgeable about similar figures with this activity!

Purpose: To construct similar figures by increasing and decreasing the size of a figure

Students will do the following:

- double the size of a figure
- halve the size of a figure

Materials for each student:

- copy of page 56
- pencil
- crayons

Vocabulary to review:

- similar figures
- half the size
- twice the size

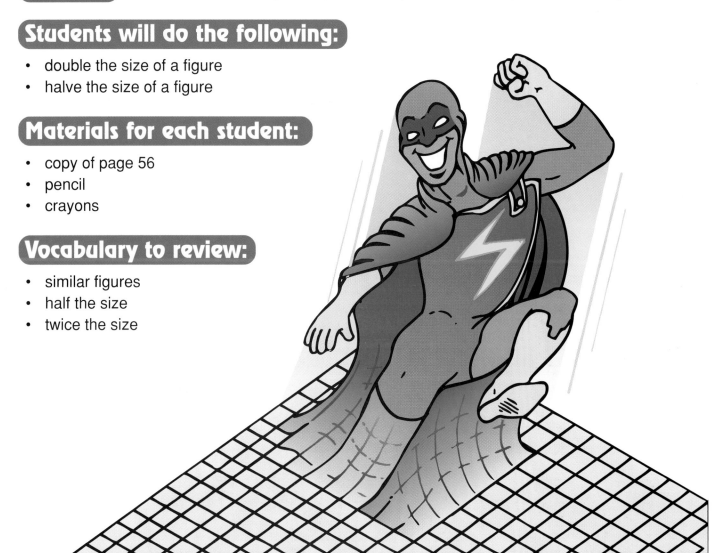

Extension activities to use after the reproducible:

- Call on the comics to give students a better understanding of similar figures. Cut apart enough comic strips to give each student one frame. Have the student glue his frame on paper and then use a ruler to draw a grid of half-inch squares that covers it. Have him also draw a grid of two-inch squares on a 12" x 18" sheet of white construction paper. Finally, have the student draw an enlarged version of the frame square by square onto his construction paper grid. Then have the student color the completed drawing.

- Connect math and reading with this supersized book-reporting idea! After each student has read her book, give her the art materials to re-create her book's cover at twice its size. Then, as she shares, the rest of the class should have no problem at all seeing her project!

Similar Figures to the Rescue!

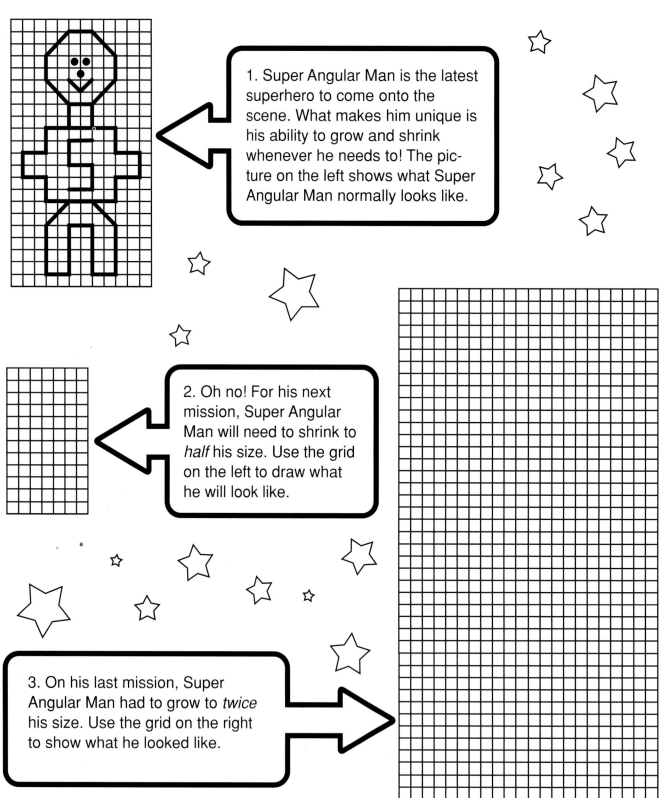

1. Super Angular Man is the latest superhero to come onto the scene. What makes him unique is his ability to grow and shrink whenever he needs to! The picture on the left shows what Super Angular Man normally looks like.

2. Oh no! For his next mission, Super Angular Man will need to shrink to *half* his size. Use the grid on the left to draw what he will look like.

3. On his last mission, Super Angular Man had to grow to *twice* his size. Use the grid on the right to show what he looked like.

Bonus Box: Draw a square and a regular hexagon on the back of this page. Measure the length of each side. Then make a drawing of each figure that is twice its original size.

Note to the teacher: Provide students with crayons for coloring the figures if desired.

Do We Have a Match?

Make this activity on congruent figures a perfect match for your students!

Purpose: To identify and construct congruent line segments, angles, and shapes

Students will do the following:

- identify given figures that are congruent
- identify congruent angles and line segments from given figures
- draw a congruent example of a given figure

Materials for each student:

- copy of page 58
- pencil
- ruler
- protractor
- yellow crayon

Vocabulary to review:

- congruent
- angles
- line segments

Extension activities to use after the reproducible:

- Turn students' own drawings of congruent figures into quick assessment tools. Give each student a ruler, scissors, glue, a sheet of drawing paper, and a sheet of white construction paper. Direct the student to construct two congruent polygons on his drawing paper, cut them out, and then mount them on the construction paper. Finally, have each child label his drawings "Congruent Figures" and then, below them, record his own definition. At a glance, you'll be able to tell who has this concept down pat!

- Help students journal their way to an understanding of similar and congruent figures. On the board, draw a pair of similar shapes. Label them "Pair A." Next to the similar shapes, draw a pair of congruent shapes. Label them "Pair B." Then instruct each student to write a paragraph in his journal comparing and contrasting these two sets of shapes.

Do We Have a Match?

Marvin and Melvin Mouse are twins who like everything to match—even their wedges of cheese! Mabel Mouse, the twins' mother, has just given them a basket of cheese wedges. Help Marvin and Melvin do some matching. Remember, figures that are *congruent* have the same shape and size. Figures that are *similar* have the same shape but not necessarily the same size. Congruent figures can also have corresponding congruent parts, such as line segments and angles.

Part I: Marvin is holding 1 wedge of cheese. Color the wedges below that are congruent to the one in Marvin's hand.

Part II: Mabel Mouse has combined several smaller wedges of cheese to make 2 larger identical wedges. Each line segment and angle in the wedge on the left corresponds to a matching part in the wedge on the right. Identify these congruent parts.

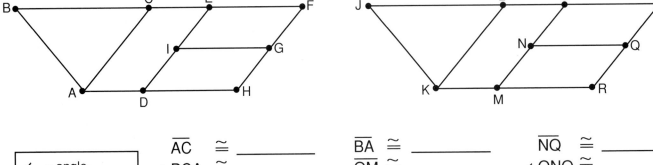

∠ = angle
— = line segment
≅ = congruent

$\overline{AC}$ ≅ _____
∠ BCA ≅ _____
∠ DHG ≅ _____
∠ OPR ≅ _____

$\overline{BA}$ ≅ _____
$\overline{OM}$ ≅ _____
$\overline{CE}$ ≅ _____
∠ JLK ≅ _____

$\overline{NQ}$ ≅ _____
∠ ONQ ≅ _____
$\overline{BF}$ ≅ _____
$\overline{KR}$ ≅ _____

Part III: Finally, study the wedge of cheese Melvin is pointing out. Then use your ruler and protractor to help you draw a congruent match for it in the space provided. Color your drawing if you wish.

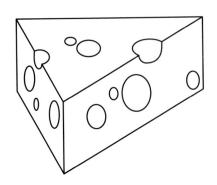

Bonus Box: On the back of this page, construct a pair of congruent trapezoids using a ruler and protractor. Measure and label each angle and line segment in your figures.

That's a Very Busy Beaver!

Here's a symmetry activity that your eager beavers can sink their teeth into!

Purpose: To create a symmetrical design

Students will do the following:

- identify spaces on a grid
- shade each space using a particular pattern
- test their design to make sure it's symmetrical

Materials for each student:

- copy of page 60
- pencil
- green crayon, pencil, or marker

Vocabulary to review:

- pattern
- coordinates
- mirror image
- symmetrical

Extension activities to use after the reproducible:

- Block out time to have students experiment with other symmetrical grid designs and to create puzzles for one another to solve. Give each student two copies of a 10 x 10 grid (see grid on page 165) and an additional sheet of plain paper. Tell each student to use one grid to create a symmetrical design of his own, using the five pattern choices shown on the reproducible. Remind each student to fold his paper on the line between the fifth and sixth columns to make sure one side of the design is a mirror image of the other. Then tell him to list the coordinates and the patterns he used on the plain paper. Finally, have students trade their lists of coordinates and use the remaining blank grids to solve one another's puzzles.

- Stretch students' understanding of symmetry by breaking out the Geoboards! Provide each student with a Geoboard and assorted rubber bands. Have each child wrap the rubber bands around the pegs to create symmetrical designs. Then provide students with Geoboard dot paper so they can re-create and color their designs on paper.

That's a Very Busy Beaver!

Mr. Rabbit is tired of the boring hedges in his garden. So he has hired Benny the Beaver to use his teeth to gnaw out a symmetrical design in the hedges! Both Benny and Mr. Rabbit know that when a symmetrical design is divided down the middle, one side is a mirror image of the other.

To find out how Mr. Rabbit's hedges look, find the following coordinates on the grid. Use a pencil to lightly shade in the squares using the pattern shown. Once you've filled in the squares, fold your paper on the line between column 5 and column 6. Is your design symmetrical? If it is, color over your pencil design in green to show the hedges. If it's not, recheck the coordinates you have shaded; then color your pencil design.

 A2, B3, C4, D5, E6, G5, J1, J3, J7, J9

 B1, C2, D3, H4

 B10, C9, D8, H7

 A9, B8, C7, D6, E5, G6, J2, J4, J8, J10

 D4, D7, E4, E7, F4, F5, F6, F7, G4, G7, H5, H6, I5, I6, J5, J6

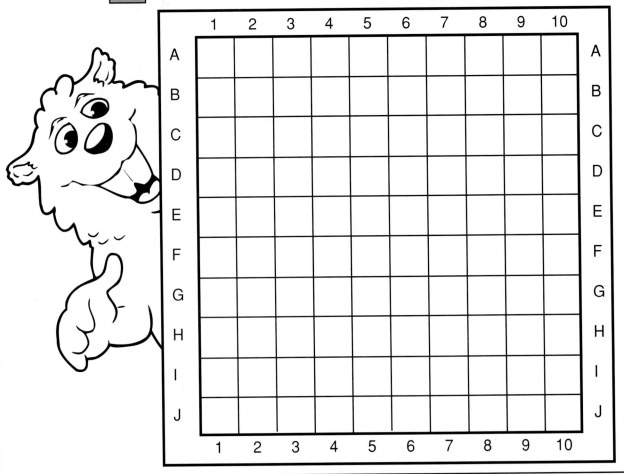

Bonus Box: Many items in nature are symmetrical. On the back of your paper, list 10 objects you might see in a park. Circle all of the items that are symmetrical.

Weaving a Study of Symmetry

Show students how symmetry plays a part in Navajo art.

Purpose: To create a symmetrical design

Students will do the following:

- examine symmetrical designs
- determine the lines of symmetry
- create their own symmetrical designs

Materials for each student:

- copy of page 62
- ruler
- pencil
- crayons or colored pencils

Vocabulary to review:

- lines of symmetry
- vertical
- horizontal
- diagonal

Extension activities to use after the reproducible:

- Roll out the red (and yellow and blue) carpet for classroom visitors and give them a chance to check out students' symmetrical designs! Have your students cut out their rug designs and mount them on matching sheets of construction paper. On the back of the paper, have the student who created the design write how many lines of symmetry the design contains. Staple only the top corners of the papers to a bulletin board titled "Welcome to Our Center of Sensational Symmetry!" Post the following directions on the bulletin board: "How many lines of symmetry do you see in each design? To check your answer, look on the back of the rug!" Invite students and classroom guests to see how their understanding of symmetry stacks up!

- To make sure students have a good grasp on symmetry, put them to the test—the mirror test, that is. Give pairs of students small mirrors, paper, and pencils. Invite your symmetry sleuths to stroll around the classroom and use the mirrors to find objects with no symmetry, one line of symmetry, two lines of symmetry, and so forth. Have each pair keep track of its findings. After ten minutes, have pairs exchange lists and check one another's findings.

Weaving a Study of Symmetry

The Navajos are known for weaving beautifully designed rugs. Many of the rugs have several lines of symmetry. If you divide the rug in half at a line of symmetry, both sides are mirror images of each other. Lines of symmetry can be vertical, horizontal, and diagonal.

Examples:

1 line of symmetry	2 lines of symmetry	4 lines of symmetry
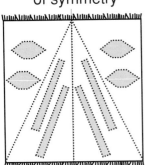		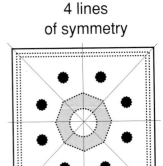

Now it's your turn to create a symmetrical design. Using the grid below, create a rug design containing at least 1 line of symmetry. Color your design.

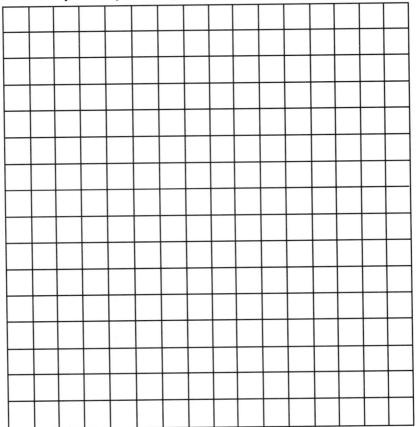

How many lines of symmetry does your design have? _____

Bonus Box: Look at the clothes you're wearing today. Are you wearing any symmetrical designs? Draw these on another sheet of paper.

Geometric Gymnastics

Slide, flip, and turn your way through this high-energy geometry lesson!

Purpose: To identify transformations: slides, flips, and turns

Students will do the following:

- label the movement of a geometric figure as a slide, a flip, or a turn
- draw examples of slides, flips, and turns

Materials for each student:

- copy of page 64
- pencil

Vocabulary to review:

- slide
- flip
- turn

Extension activities to use after the reproducible:

- Help students identify slides, flips, and turns in real-life activities. Write the following sentences on the board:
    1. A skier skiing down a hill is an example of a _____. *(slide)*
    2. A skier doing a somersault off a ski jump is an example of a _____. *(flip)*
    3. An ice-skater spinning on one foot is an example of a _____. *(turn)*

    Have the students complete each sentence. Then have each student make a list of other real-life situations that demonstrate each movement.

- Making turns is as easy as *A, B, C* with the following activity! Provide each student with one large sheet of white construction paper, a stencil of the first letter of his name, and crayons or markers. Direct the student to place the stencil at the top of the construction paper and then trace it. Then have the student turn the stencil 90 degrees and trace it in its new position. Have the student turn the stencil two more 90-degree turns, tracing it in its new position each time. Next, have the student return the stencil to its beginning position and continue the design with a series of 45-degree turns. Instruct the student to trace the stencil at each turn. Finally, have the student use markers or crayons to color his completed design.

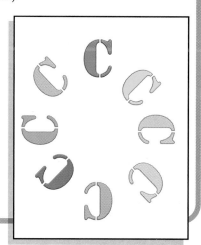

Name _____

Geometric Gymnastics

Tabby Tumbler and her friends have learned 3 new moves in gymnastics class: slides, flips, and turns. Look at the examples below. Then identify each move correctly.

Examples:

Slide	**Flip**	**Turn**
	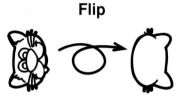	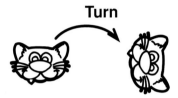
The figure moves along a straight line.	The figure flips over a line.	The figure moves around a point.

1. _____

2. _____

3. _____

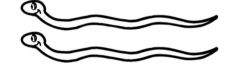

4. _____

5. _____

6. _____

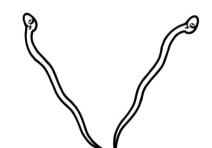

7. _____

8. _____

9. _____

Bonus Box: Help Tabby with her geometric gymnastic moves by sliding, flipping, and turning each letter in her name. Show your work on the back of this page.

©2001 The Education Center, Inc. • *Math Skills Workout* • TEC3229 • Key p. 170

Mapping Out a Mystery

Have your students solve the mystery of coordinate graphing with this activity!

Purpose: To use coordinates to locate and plot points on a grid

Students will do the following:

- use coordinates to plot points on a grid
- connect points on a grid to create a picture
- match coordinates with letters on a grid to solve the mystery

Materials for each student:

- copy of page 66
- pencil

Vocabulary to review:

- coordinates
- ordered pair
- plot

Extension activities to use after the reproducible:

- Give students more practice with coordinate graphing with the following activity. Provide each student with a 10 x 10 grid (see grid on page 165). Direct the student to plot all the letters of the alphabet on his graph. Then instruct the student to write each of his spelling words using the coordinates he plotted. Have the student trade papers with a partner and decipher the coded words.

- Help students make the connection between math and geography with the following activity. For each student, duplicate a world map that has latitude and longitude lines on it. Have students identify specific sites on the map—such as countries, cities, and bodies of water—located nearest to a pair of longitude and latitude coordinates. For example, Bolivia would be nearest to the coordinate pair (60°W longitude, 20°S latitude).

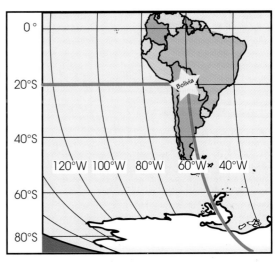

Mapping Out a Mystery

Famous writer Agatha MacChristie has hired Detective Sherlock McHurlock to investigate the mystery of her missing manuscript. Use your knowledge of coordinate graphing to help Detective McHurlock uncover the clues to the mystery. First, find out where the manuscript was last seen by plotting the coordinates on the grid below to draw an object. Then answer the question at the bottom of the page by matching the coordinates to the letters on the corresponding grid.

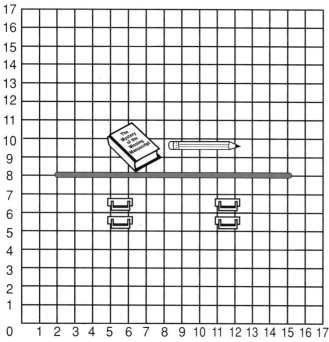

The missing manuscript was last seen on Miss MacChristie's _____.

Directions: Graph each group of coordinates below on the grid at the left. For example, to graph (3, 4), start at 0. Count 3 spaces to the right; then count 4 spaces up. Make a dot. In the same way, make a dot for the next coordinate. Draw a line to connect the 2 points. Plot the points in group A and connect them with lines in that order. Continue with group B. Then complete the picture by plotting and connecting the points in group C.

Group A

(3, 11), (2, 8), (3, 4), (4, 4), (4, 3), (5, 3), (5, 4), (12, 4), (12, 3), (13, 3), (13, 4), (14, 4), (15, 8), (14, 11), (3, 11)

Group B

(4, 7), (4, 5), (7, 5), (7, 7), (4, 7)

Group C

(10, 7), (10, 5), (13, 5), (13, 7), (10, 7)

Directions: Use the coordinates below and the grid at the right to solve the mystery below.

Where was the missing manuscript found?

in the ___ ___ ___ ___ ___ ___ ___ ___ ___ ___
(7, 9) (1, 1) (1, 8) (8, 5) (7, 9) (9, 7) (4, 4) (1, 4) (1, 1) (9, 7)

Bonus Box: Write a secret message on the back of this page. Draw a blank line for each letter in the message. Under each blank, write the ordered pair from the lettered grid at the right that matches each letter. Then have a classmate use the grid and your clues to read the message.

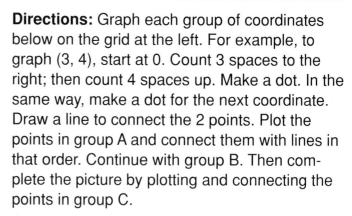

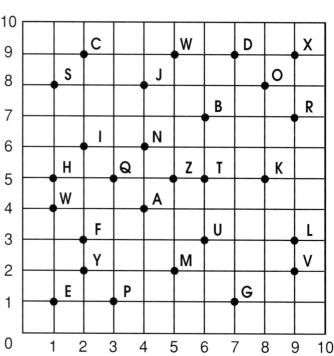

Coordinating Pictures

Have your students create their own coordinate-graphing works of art with this activity!

Purpose: To design and construct an original picture using coordinate pairs

Students will do the following:

- design and create a picture by plotting and connecting coordinate pairs
- follow a classmate's list of coordinate pairs to recreate a drawing

Materials for each student:

- copy of page 68
- pencil

Vocabulary to review:

- coordinates
- grid

Extension activities to use after the reproducible:

- Transform your students into expert decoding sleuths with this point-plotting activity for partners. Give each student one copy of a large, labeled quadrant. Have each student plot all the letters of the alphabet on his quadrant. Then instruct one student to write a message to his partner using the coordinates he plotted. Direct the partner to use the coordinates to decipher the coded message. As a variation, allow students to use the quadrants for practicing their spelling and vocabulary words.

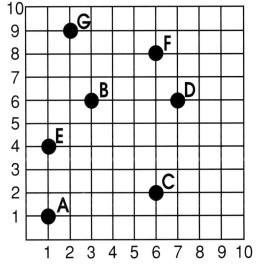

- Have students practice their coordinate-graphing skills with this research activity. Divide your students into small groups. Number each group and give each group a thermometer, a sheet of graph paper, and a sheet of drawing paper. Instruct each group to write its assigned number on the sheet of drawing paper. Then have each group place the thermometer on its numbered paper in a safe location outside the classroom. Then have a different member of each group check the temperature reading on its thermometer each hour during the day. The next day, have each group track the temperature readings for the previous day by creating a line graph and plotting the information on the grid. Have each group present its completed grid to the rest of the class. Then have the class compare the findings of each group.

Coordinating Pictures

Try your hand at designing a picture that can be formed by connecting points on a grid.

Part I: Create your picture by marking 20 different points on the grid below and recording the coordinate pairs for each point in the space provided to the left of the grid. Be sure to list the coordinate pairs in the order in which they should be connected. Then connect the dots to reveal your picture.

Coordinate Pairs

1. _____ 11. _____
2. _____ 12. _____
3. _____ 13. _____
4. _____ 14. _____
5. _____ 15. _____
6. _____ 16. _____
7. _____ 17. _____
8. _____ 18. _____
9. _____ 19. _____
10. _____ 20. _____

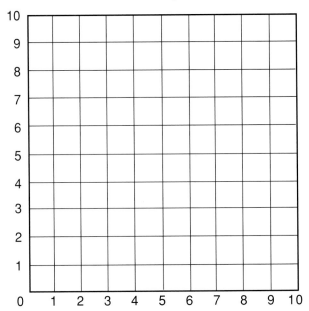

- -

Part II: Have a friend re-create your drawing by following your coordinates. Carefully rewrite each pair of coordinates in the correct order below. Fold the top part of this paper back along the dotted line so that the drawing above cannot be seen. Then exchange papers with a friend and see who can best re-create the other's drawing.

Coordinate Pairs

1. _____ 11. _____
2. _____ 12. _____
3. _____ 13. _____
4. _____ 14. _____
5. _____ 15. _____
6. _____ 16. _____
7. _____ 17. _____
8. _____ 18. _____
9. _____ 19. _____
10. _____ 20. _____

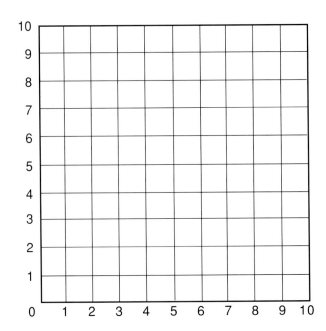

Triangle Trios

Help your students see that learning about triangles is as easy as 1-2-3!

Purpose: To identify and make equilateral, isosceles, and scalene triangles

Students will do the following:

- make multiple examples of equilateral, isosceles, and scalene triangles
- combine examples of the three kinds of triangles into an art design

Materials for each student:

- copy of page 70
- pencil
- ruler
- protractor
- crayons or colored markers

Vocabulary to review:

- equilateral triangle
- isosceles triangle
- scalene triangle

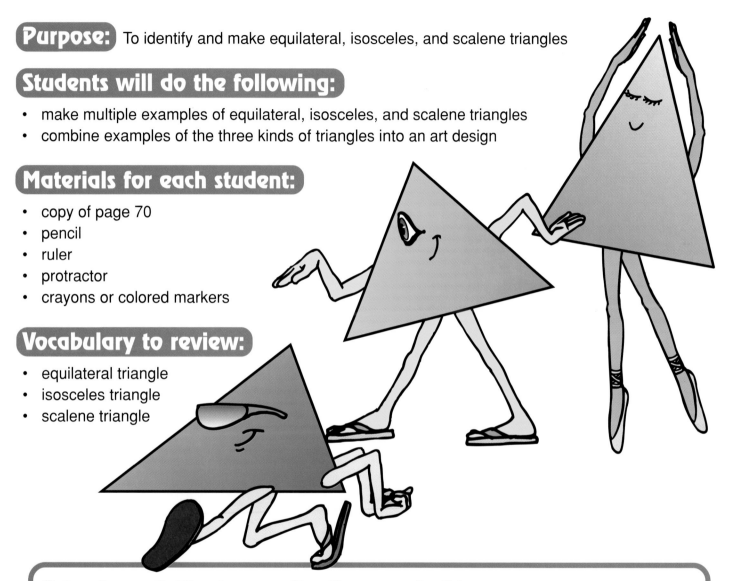

Extension activities to use after the reproducible:

- Provide each student with about 20 toothpicks. Have each student use the toothpicks to make an equilateral triangle on a sheet of paper or on her desk. Make sure that each student labels the number of toothpicks used for each side of the triangle. Invite students to share their toothpick examples on an overhead projector as well. Repeat this activity with isosceles and scalene triangles.

- Play Triango! First, make a spinner that has three sections and label them "equilateral," "isosceles," and "scalene." Next, have each student fold a sheet of paper in half four times and then unfold it. Direct the student to draw examples of the three kinds of triangles in the 16 boxes on his sheet, one triangle per box. To play, spin the spinner and call out the kind of triangle it points to. Direct each student to find a matching triangle on his game sheet and write "1" on it. Spin again and call out the triangle that the spinner points to; then direct each student to write "2" on a matching triangle on his sheet. (Jot down the numbers and triangle types so that you'll have a key.) Continue play until a student has marked four triangles in a row and calls out "Triango!"

Triangle Trios

Trina Triangle loves to create artwork using the shapes she knows best—triangles, of course! Today she is focusing on *equilateral, isosceles,* and *scalene* triangles. Check out the definition of each one on the easel.

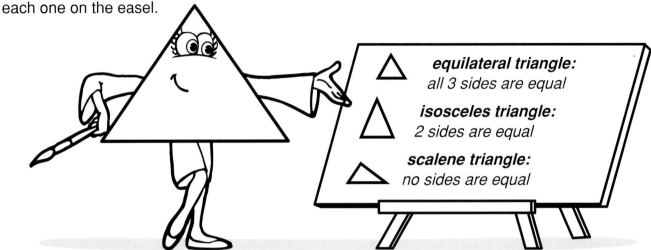

equilateral triangle:
all 3 sides are equal

isosceles triangle:
2 sides are equal

scalene triangle:
no sides are equal

Help Trina create her triangle design in the space below. Will you design a far-out space vehicle? A new and different piece of playground equipment? A futuristic home?

Include at least 5 examples of each kind of triangle in the design. Arrange the triangles in any way that you wish. Have fun and be creative!

Bonus Box: List 5 real-life objects that have triangle shapes.

A Garden Full of Circles

Encourage students' creativity and plant new geometric skills with this task!

Purpose: To create an art scene that includes circles of different sizes

Students will do the following:

- make circles of different radii and diameters
- measure in inches and centimeters

Materials for each student:

- copy of page 72
- pencil
- ruler
- compass
- crayons or colored markers
- 12" x 18" sheet of white construction paper

Vocabulary to review:

- radius/radii
- diameter
- circumference

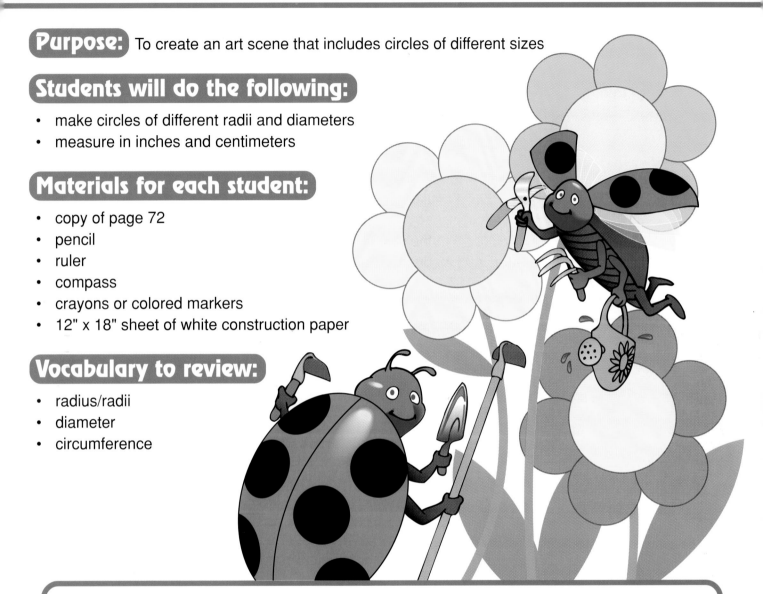

Extension activities to use after the reproducible:

- Help students understand the relationship between the diameter and circumference of a circle with this group activity. In advance, ask students to bring in a variety of objects shaped like circles (examples: jar lids, margarine tub lids, components of games, Frisbee® disks, paper plates, Hula-Hoop® plastic rings). Divide students into small groups and provide each group with three or four items. First, have students predict the circumference of each item. Then have the students in each group use string and a ruler to measure both the diameter and circumference of each circle shape. When they're finished, ask students to describe the relationship between each circle's diameter and its circumference. *(The circumference of any circle is approximately three times its diameter.)*

- Have students create circle designs using compasses. Direct each student to include in her design circles that have specific measurements. For example, include two circles, each with a diameter of five centimeters; also include three circles, each with a diameter of two inches.

A Garden Full of Circles

Your knowledge of circles will bloom as you create this geometric garden! Read and follow the directions below very carefully. When you're finished, you'll have a true work of art—*and math!*

Part I: Make a garden scene on your sheet of construction paper. Include and label each of the following:

    a. a flower whose center has a radius of $\frac{1}{2}$"

    b. a flower whose center has a radius of 1"

    c. a flower whose center has a diameter of 3"

    d. a caterpillar with 5 circular parts (including the head); each part has a diameter of 2 cm

    e. the sun with a radius of 4 cm

    f. a ladybug whose body has a diameter of 4 cm

When you've completed all 10 circles, add extra things to your garden to make a complete picture. Then use crayons or markers to color your garden.

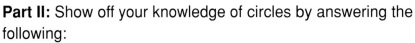

Part II: Show off your knowledge of circles by answering the following:

    a. What is the diameter of a circle whose radius is 12 inches? _____ Explain. _____
_____
_____

    b. What is the radius of a circle whose diameter is 14 centimeters? _____ Explain. _____
_____
_____

    c. On the back of this sheet, use a compass to draw a circle with a radius of 4 centimeters. Estimate the circumference of the circle. _____

    d. The circumference of any circle is approximately 3.14 times its diameter. What is the approximate circumference of the circle you drew? _____

    e. How close was your estimate (part c) to the circumference (part d) of your circle? _____

Bonus Box: Which circle has a greater circumference: one with a radius of 5 cm or one with a diameter of 8 cm? Explain.

Doin' the Tessellation Slide

Use this creative activity to give students fun practice with tessellations!

Purpose: To create a tessellated design

Students will do the following:

- make a straight-line stencil
- make repeated slides with the stencil
- trace the stencil after each slide
- complete a full page of tessellations

Materials for each student:

- copy of page 74
- pencil
- 3" tagboard square
- scissors
- crayons
- tape
- 12" x 18" sheet of white construction paper

Vocabulary to review:

- stencil
- slide
- tessellation

Extension activities to use after the reproducible:

- Challenge students to create stencils with curved lines to follow up the reproducible activity on page 74. Give each student the materials needed from the list above. Then direct him to follow the directions on page 74 again, but this time drawing a curved line instead of a straight one. Display the resulting tessellations on a board titled "Doin' the Tessellation Slide!"

- Fill an entire bulletin board with tessellations! Cover the board with white paper. Near the board, place a stencil made from an eight-inch tagboard square. Have students take turns sliding and tracing the stencil until the board's background is covered completely. Next, help students decide how to color the tracings in an attractive manner. When the coloring has been completed, have each student write his own definition of a tessellation and a step-by-step explanation of how the class produced this giant tessellation.

Doin' the Tessellation Slide

Are you ready to do the tessellation slide? Just follow the directions below to create a stencil. Then you can *really* start to slide!

1. Write "Up" on one side of your tagboard square. This will help you remember to keep this side up as you work.

2. Using straight cuts, carefully cut a section from the top of the square as shown.

3. Slide the cutout section to the bottom of the square. (Do not flip it!) Match the edges; then tape them securely.

4. Cut a section from the left side of the square as shown.

5. Slide the cutout section to the right side of the square. (Do not flip it!) Match the edges; then tape them securely.

6. Place the stencil in the center of the white paper.

7. Trace the stencil with a pencil.

8. Slide the stencil (up, down, right, or left) and match its edge with the tracing. Make another tracing.

9. Continue sliding and tracing until your paper is covered completely with tracings.

10. Look at the tessellated shape in the center. Add details to it, such as dots, lines, geometric shapes, or a face. Make sure you add the same details to each of the other tessellated shapes.

11. Color the tessellations, outlining each one with a black crayon.

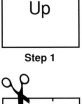

Step 1

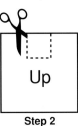

Step 2

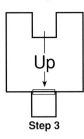

Step 3

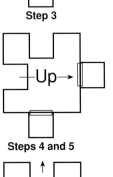

Steps 4 and 5

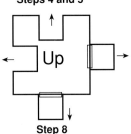

Step 8

Bonus Box: Choose any pattern block to tessellate on the back of this page. Cover the page completely with your tracings. Add the same details to each tracing. Then color the tessellations.

Ice-Cream Outcomes

Purpose: To find probability

Students will do the following:

- identify possible outcomes
- make predictions
- conduct a probability experiment
- complete a frequency table
- interpret data from a frequency table
- write to explain their thinking

Materials for each student:

- copy of page 76
- paper clip and pencil

Vocabulary to review:

- possible outcomes
- probability
- most likely, least likely, equally likely
- experiment
- frequency
- tally

Extension activities to use after the reproducible:

- Show students that working with probability can be a real treat! Create a large spinner using a piece of tagboard, a large paper clip, and a pencil. Divide the spinner into six equal sections, labeling three of the sections "sticker," two sections "candy," and one section "free time." With the class, identify all the possible outcomes, the probability of spinning each outcome, and a most likely and least likely outcome. Then conduct a class experiment to test the predictions. In turn, have a different student spin the spinner for a total of 20 times. Record the results in a frequency table on the chalkboard. After discussing the results, use the spinner to choose a treat to share with your probability-seeking students!

- Put probability in the bag with this activity! Divide students into small groups. Provide each group with a bag of various pattern blocks. Direct each group to remove the blocks from its bag and sort them. Ask each group to identify all the possible outcomes of selecting each type of block and which block(s) is most likely or least likely to be selected. After replacing the blocks, instruct group members to take turns picking and replacing blocks for a total of 20 times. Have each group record its results on a frequency table, then share its findings.

Ice-Cream Outcomes

Ivan, the ice-cream man, is busy all day making neighborhood stops. Because his stops are quick, he designed a spinner to help his customers decide which cool treat to select. Put Ivan's idea to the test by completing each item below.

 Identify all the *possible outcomes* (all the possible treats that may be selected) from the spinner.

_____

 What is the *probability* (chance of something happening) of spinning each outcome?

Popsicle® _____ out of 8   ice-cream cone _____ out of 8

PUSH UP® pop _____ out of 8   Italian ice _____ out of 8

 Which treat(s) is most likely to be selected? _____

Least likely? _____   Equally likely? _____

 If Ivan has 20 customers who need to use the spinner, predict the number of times each outcome could be spun. (Round the answer to the nearest whole number.)

Popsicle _____   ice-cream cone _____

PUSH UP pop _____   Italian ice _____

 Conduct an experiment to see if your predictions are correct. Spin the spinner 20 times. Record the results of each spin in the frequency table below. Mark a tally in the correct column for each spin. Then record the frequency (total number) of each tally.

Type of Treat	Tally	Frequency
Popsicle		
PUSH UP pop		
ice-cream cone		
Italian ice		

 Do the results of your experiment match your predictions? Explain your answer on the back of this sheet.

Note to the teacher: To use the spinner, direct the student to place a paper clip in the center and use the point of a pencil to hold it in place while spinning it.

Horsing Around With Probability

Make predicting probability a "shoe-in" with this activity!

Purpose: To predict probability using a frequency table

Students will do the following:

- organize a set of numbers by selecting appropriate intervals
- complete a frequency table
- interpret data from a frequency table
- write to explain their thinking

Materials for each student:

- copy of page 78
- pencil

Vocabulary to review:

- interval
- range
- frequency table
- most likely
- least likely

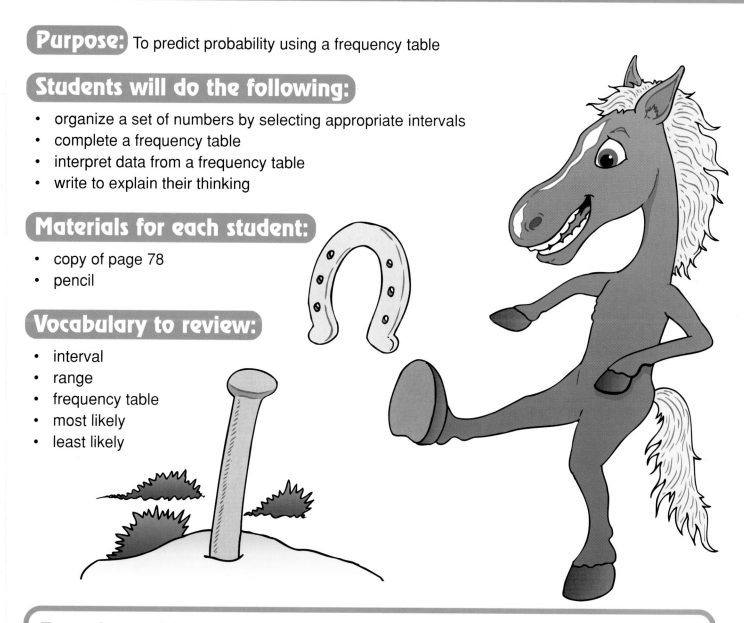

Extension activities to use after the reproducible:

- Challenge students in the "sport" of making frequency tables! Divide students into groups and give each group a copy of scores from the sports section of your local newspaper. Direct each group to highlight the winning scores. Have the group identify appropriate intervals for the scores and then organize the information in a frequency table.

- Combine a nutritious snack with making and interpreting frequency tables. Provide each pair of students with a snack box of raisins. Direct each pair to count the number of raisins in its box and then report this number to you. As a class, organize the numbers into appropriate intervals and then create a frequency table organizing the information. Have student pairs take turns asking one another questions that can be answered by interpreting the data on the table. While asking and answering questions, invite students to snack away on their raisins!

Horsing Around With Probability

Harry and his pals love to pitch horseshoes! They have just finished playing in their annual team tournament. This year Harry is in charge of awarding ribbons. Harry needs to organize the scores by intervals so he can do this. Help Harry organize the scores in the 5 categories shown.

1. Study the scores listed on the Shoe Sheet below. Decide how Harry can organize the scores into 5 different *intervals,* or ranges, such as 0–9, 10–19, etc. Then assign an interval to each place category listed.

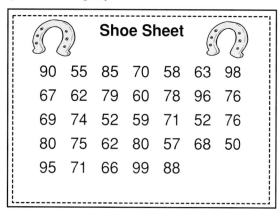

Shoe Sheet

90	55	85	70	58	63	98
67	62	79	60	78	96	76
69	74	52	59	71	52	76
80	75	62	80	57	68	50
95	71	66	99	88

First Place: _____

Second Place: _____

Third Place: _____

Fourth Place: _____

Honorable Mention: _____

2. Help Harry organize the information by filling in the frequency table below.

Place	Interval	Tally	Frequency

3. How many players scored in the fourth place range? _____

4. How many scores are there in all? _____

5. How many more players scored in the third place range than in the second place range?

_____

6. For which place is Harry *most likely* to award a ribbon and why? _____

_____

For which place is Harry *least likely* to award a ribbon and why? _____

_____

Bonus Box: On the back of this sheet, write 2 questions that can be answered by interpreting the data in the frequency table above. Then give your questions to another classmate to answer.

It All Adds Up!

Put students' success in the cards with this activity!

Purpose To find probability using number cards

Students will do the following:

- make predictions
- conduct a probability experiment
- find and record sums of numbers

Materials for each pair of students:

- copy of page 80
- pencil
- set of index cards labeled 1–6
- paper lunch bag

Vocabulary to review:

- tree diagram
- possible outcomes
- probability

Extension activities to use after the reproducible:

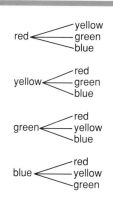

- Put tree diagrams on deck with this probability activity! Place the following items at a center: four colored counters—one red, one yellow, one green, and one blue; a paper lunch bag; a pencil; and a supply of loose-leaf paper. In turn, send student pairs to the center. Direct each pair to construct a tree diagram showing all the possible outcomes of choosing a pair of counters. Then have them identify the probability of picking a pair such as a red and yellow (²/₁₂ or ¹/₆) or blue and green (²/₁₂ or ¹/₆). Then have each pair conduct an experiment, picking two counters from the bag for 20 turns. After each turn, have the pair return the counters, record the results on a frequency table, and then compare the table with the tree diagram answers.

- Put a spin on probability with this game for two. Pair students and provide each pair with a sheet of construction paper, a paper clip, and a pencil. Direct each pair to create a spinner labeled *1, 2, 3,* and *4.* In turn, have each player spin the spinner twice, add the two numbers, and record the sum on a loose-leaf sheet of paper. After 20 rounds, instruct each player to circle all his sums of five. The winner is the player with the most sums of five. Follow up the game by asking students what the probability of spinning a sum of five is *(⁴/₁₆)* and if their experiments proved this true.

Names _____

    # It All Adds Up!

The Kitty Card Company has just released its newest game—Six and Up. Try a hand (or paw!) at this game by following the directions below. Then, with your partner, complete the items that follow.

Directions for 2 players:

1. Player 1 picks 2 cards out of the bag.
2. Player 1 records the numbers of the cards picked and the sum of the numbers in the chart at the left. The cards are then returned to the bag.
3. Player 2 takes a turn in the same manner, recording the numbers in the chart at the right.
4. Play continues for 20 rounds. The player with the most sums of 6 or higher is the winner.

Player 1

Turn	Card 1	Card 2	Sum	Turn	Card 1	Card 2	Sum
1				11			
2				12			
3				13			
4				14			
5				15			
6				16			
7				17			
8				18			
9				19			
10				20			

Player 2

Turn	Card 1	Card 2	Sum	Turn	Card 1	Card 2	Sum
1				11			
2				12			
3				13			
4				14			
5				15			
6				16			
7				17			
8				18			
9				19			
10				20			

1. On the back of this sheet, construct a tree diagram showing all the possible outcomes for picking 2 cards from the bag.

2. How many possible outcomes are there? _____

3. What is the probability of picking 2 cards with a sum of 6 or higher? _____

4. What is the probability of picking 2 cards with a sum of 5 or less? _____

Bonus Box: If a card labeled with the number 7 was added to the bag, how many additional outcomes would there be?

On a Roll With Probability

Help your students roll into a better understanding of the fairness of a game!

Purpose: To determine the fairness of a game

Students will do the following:

- identify odd and even products
- conduct a probability experiment
- complete a frequency table
- identify possible outcomes
- determine the fairness of a game
- write to explain their thinking

$6 \times 5 = 30$

Materials for each pair of students:

- copy of page 82
- pencil
- 2 number cubes (numbered 1–6) or 2 copies of the cube pattern on page 166 (numbered 1–6)
- scissors
- glue or tape

Vocabulary to review:

- odd/even products
- more likely
- equally likely

Extension activities to use after the reproducible:

- After students complete page 82, have each pair conduct an experiment to determine the probability of rolling an odd or an even sum using both number cubes (*18/36 for either*). Direct the pair to roll the cube 40 times, recording the results on a frequency table. If desired, have the pair transfer the data to a bar graph.

- Put a little color into the probability equation! Pair students and give each pair two copies of the cube pattern on page 166. Have the pair color each space on the blank cube with a different color and then construct the cubes as directed on the page. Ask students questions such as "What is the likelihood of rolling an odd number paired with each color?" (*3/36*) or "An even number paired with each color?" (*3/36*) Then have the pair roll the cube 40 times to test its prediction, recording the results of each roll on a frequency table.

82

On a Roll With Probability

Professor I. M. Square has designed a new game for his math students called Odds and Evens. Before the class can play, the professor must determine if the game is fair. Complete Parts I and II below to help Professor Square make his decision.

Part I: Play the game according to the directions. Record the outcome of each turn on the frequency table. Then check "Yes" or "No" telling whether you feel the game is fair.

Directions for 2 players:
1. Decide who will be Player 1 and Player 2.
2. In turn, Players 1 and 2 roll the number cubes.
3. If the product of the numbers rolled is odd, Player 1 receives 1 point. Player 2 receives a point if the product is even.
4. After rolling the number cubes a total of 40 times, the player with more points wins the game.

Frequency Table

Player/Product	Tally	Frequency
Player 1/Odd		
Player 2/Even		

Yes   No

Part II: Complete the product table below. (The first row is done for you.) Circle all of the even products.

Product Table

	1	2	3	4	5	6
1	1	2	3	4	5	6
2						
3						
4						
5						
6						

1. Based on the information in the product table, is an odd or an even product more likely to be rolled? Explain. _____
_____
_____

2. Based on the information in the product table, do you think this game is fair? _____ Is this answer different from your first answer? Explain. _____
_____

Bonus Box: If you were using just 1 cube, which would you most likely roll—an odd or an even number? Explain your answer on the back of this sheet.

Note to the teacher: Have the pair follow the directions on page 166 for constructing the cubes before playing the game.

Matches and Mismatches

Have your students quacking about the fairness of a math game with this activity!

Purpose: To determine the fairness of a game

Students will do the following:

- make an organized list
- identify possible outcomes
- make predictions
- conduct a probability experiment
- complete a frequency table
- interpret data
- determine the fairness of a game
- write to explain their thinking

Materials for each student:

- copy of page 84
- paper clip
- pencil

Vocabulary to review:

- match and mismatch
- organized list
- possible combinations
- experiment
- frequency table
- tally

Extension activities to use after the reproducible:

- Get your students screaming for additional probability practice using some tasty combinations! Copy the list below onto a transparency or a chalkboard. Divide students into small groups. Instruct each group to work together to make an organized list of all the possible ice-cream sundaes that could be made using one choice from each group. *(There are a total of 27 possible combinations.)* After each group has developed its list, ask questions such as "What is the probability of having a sundae with chocolate chips?" *($^9/_{27}$)* or "What is the probability of having a sundae with caramel and sprinkles?" *($^3/_{27}$)*

chocolate	hot fudge	nuts
strawberry	caramel	sprinkles
vanilla	peanut butter	chocolate chips

- Give student pairs more practice with the probability of combinations. Provide each pair of students with two dice or two number cubes (numbered 1–6). Direct each pair to make an organized list of all the possible combinations available on the pair of dice or cubes. *(There are a total of 36 possible combinations.)* As a class, review the lists and then identify the probability of rolling doubles *($^6/_{36}$)*. Next, instruct each pair to conduct an experiment to test the prediction. Have partners roll the two dice or cubes for a total of 40 times and record the results on a frequency table; then, as a class, discuss the results.

Matches and Mismatches

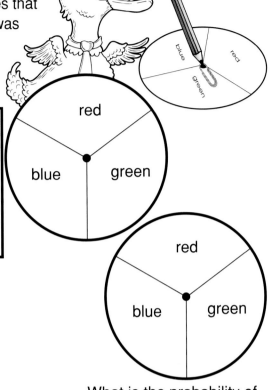

The Quacko Toy Company recently produced some games that weren't very fair. The company's president, I. M. Quackers, was accused of being a quack! Mr. Quackers has asked that you review his newest game. Complete the items below to help the president decide if he should sell the game.

Game Rules
1. In turn, Player 1 and Player 2 spin both spinners.
2. Player 1 earns a point when a *match* is spun (2 of the same color). Player 2 earns a point when a *mismatch* is spun (2 different colors).
3. After 20 total spins, the player with the most points wins the game.

1. Make an organized list of the possible outcomes of the 2 spinners.

2. How many possible outcomes are there? _____ What is the probability of spinning a match with the 2 spinners? _____ A mismatch? _____

3. Conduct an experiment to test the fairness of the game. Follow the directions for playing the game, spinning the spinner for both Players 1 and 2. Record the results on the frequency table below.

Colors	Tally	Frequency
Match		
Mismatch		

4. If you were playing the game with a partner, would you choose to be Player 1 or Player 2? Explain.

_____
_____
_____

5. On the back of this sheet, write a letter to the president of Quacko Toy Company telling him whether he should sell the game. Explain how you arrived at your decision, including details about the activities you completed.

Bonus Box: If the colors on the spinners were changed to those shown at the right, would Player 1 have a more likely chance of winning the game? Why or why not? Write your answer on the back of this sheet.	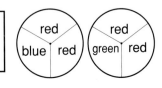

©2001 The Education Center, Inc. • *Math Skills Workout* • TEC3229 • Key p. 171

Statistics to the Rescue!

Save your students from the danger of unorganized data!

Purpose: To collect and organize data

Students will do the following:

- collect data
- display data on a frequency table
- construct a bar graph
- interpret data

Materials for each student:

- copy of page 86
- pencil

Vocabulary to review:

- survey
- frequency table
- data
- bar graph
- most likely
- least likely
- equally likely

Extension activities to use after the reproducible:

- Your students will get the scoop on statistics with this activity! Obtain similar-sized paragraphs from a local newspaper. Pair students and provide each pair with a paragraph. Ask each pair to predict whether there are more vowels or more consonants in the text. Then direct each pair to count the number of vowels and consonants in its paragraph, recording the results on a frequency table. As a class, discuss each pair's results and whether its predictions matched its data.

- Give your lesson on statistics some taste! Divide students into pairs or small groups. Direct the students in each group to wash their hands; then give the group a small bag of M&M's® candies and a napkin or paper towel. Instruct the group to sort its candies by color, recording the results on a frequency table. Then have each group write a paragraph explaining the results of the data it collected. After sharing its data, invite each group to eat the candies.

Statistics to the Rescue!

Career Day is coming up at school, and your teacher has invited 3 emergency workers to visit your class. Unfortunately, there is only enough time for 1 worker to speak. Which one should it be: Firefighter Frank, Police Officer Pete, or Paramedic Polly? Help your teacher make a decision by completing the items below.

1. Survey your classmates to find out which job each finds most interesting. Record the results on the frequency table at the right.

2. Display your data on the bar graph below.

Frequency Table

Job	Tally	Frequency
firefighter		
police officer		
paramedic		

Title

Number of Students

22
20
18
16
14
12
10
8
6
4
2
0

Jobs

3. Which emergency worker is most likely to be chosen by your teacher? Explain.

_____

_____

_____

4. Which emergency worker is least likely to be chosen by your teacher? Explain.

_____

_____

_____

5. Are there any workers who are equally likely to be chosen? Which ones?

_____

_____

_____

Bonus Box: On the back of this sheet, write 3 sentences explaining why you think collecting data was a fair or unfair way to choose a guest speaker.

Crazy for Cookies

Bake up some delicious results with this statistics activity!

Purpose: To calculate the mean, median, mode, and range of given data

Students will do the following:

- calculate mean, median, mode, and range
- interpret data

Materials for each student:

- copy of page 88
- pencil

Vocabulary to review:

- mean
- median
- mode
- range

Extension activities to use after the reproducible:

- Have students put their math scores to the test—statistically speaking! Give each student the scores from her last five math assignments. Direct each student to calculate the mean of these scores. Then, in her math journal, have each student explain how she arrived at her answer. If desired, also have the student write what she can do to maintain or improve this score.

- Lead a discussion with students about how statistics are used in other areas of everyday life. Have students give examples, such as in batting averages, average rainfall, populations, and temperatures. Then divide students into small groups. Give each group a set of numbers from newspapers, such as the recorded temperatures from the last five days or sports teams' scores. Have the group find the mean, median, mode, and range for the set of numbers.

Crazy for Cookies

Mr. M. Mouse's class had a cookie sale to raise money for new playground equipment. Use the information in the chart below to calculate the *mean, median, mode,* and *range* of each student's total number of boxes sold. Then answer the questions that follow.

Remember:

- *Mean* is the sum of a set of numbers divided by how many numbers are in the set.
- *Median* is the middle number when the set of numbers is listed in order from least to greatest.
- *Mode* is the number that occurs most often.
- *Range* is the difference between the greatest number and the least number in a set of numbers.

	Oatmeal Raisin	Chocolate Chip	Sugar	Peanut Butter	Mint	Mean	Median	Mode	Range
Minnie	8	15	10	5	12				
Marty	4	10	13	7	16				
Molly	7	4	8	8	13				
Michael	8	8	15	8	6				
Milton	6	11	7	7	9				
Monty	6	20	13	9	12				
Mandy	7	18	10	13	7				
Mabel	6	16	5	8	5				
Mary	3	8	6	6	2				
Merwin	5	10	13	9	8				

1. Which student has the highest mean in number of boxes sold? _____

2. Which student has the lowest mean in number of boxes sold? _____

3. Which students have the same mean in number of boxes sold? _____

4. Is the mean number of boxes sold higher for Mandy or Merwin? _____

5. What is the median number of boxes sold by Molly? _____

6. What is the mode of the number of boxes sold by Milton? _____

7. What is the range of the number of boxes sold by Michael? _____

8. Does Mabel or Minnie have the greater range in number of boxes sold? _____

Bonus Box: Use the information in the chart to answer the following questions: Which cookie has the highest mean in number of boxes sold? Which cookie has the lowest mean in number of boxes sold? Write your answers on the back of this sheet.

Just Your Average Family

Get your students relating to statistics with this activity!

Purpose: To calculate the mean, median, mode, and range of data collected

Students will do the following:

- collect and organize data
- calculate mean, median, mode, and range
- interpret data

Materials for each student:

- copy of page 90
- pencil

Vocabulary to review:

- mean
- median
- mode
- range

Extension activities to use after the reproducible:

- Statistics a game? You bet! Give each student a number cube (numbered 1–6), or have him construct a cube from the pattern on page 166. Direct each student to roll the cube ten times, recording the results on a sheet of paper. Challenge the student to calculate the mean of the ten rolls. Have each student call out his mean score; then record the highest score on a chalkboard. Explain that this score (and student) wins the round. Play several rounds, as desired. Then, as a class, calculate the mean, median, mode, and range of the set of numbers on the chalkboard.

- Ever wonder exactly how many candies come in a package? Challenge your students to find the answer. Give each pair of students a small bag of the same kind of candy, such as M&M's® or Reese's Pieces® candies. Have each pair count the total number of candies in its bag. Record the results on a chalkboard. Then have each pair calculate the mean, median, mode, and range of the set of numbers on the chalkboard. (Provide students with calculators, if necessary.) Follow up the activity by inviting students to eat their "statistical" snacks.

Just Your Average Family

So just how average is your family? Complete the items below to find out!

1. On the chart below, write the name and number of family members of each student in your group.

Student's Name	Number of Family Members

2. Calculate the mean, median, mode, and range of this set of numbers. Write a number sentence showing how you got your answer.

Mean _____

Median _____

Mode _____

Range _____

3. On the chart below, record the mean number of family members for each group in your class.

Group Number	Mean Number of Family Members

4. Calculate the mean, median, mode, and range of this set of numbers. Write a number sentence showing how you got your answer.

Mean _____

Median _____

Mode _____

Range _____

Note to the teacher: Divide students into groups of 5 prior to beginning this activity. Record the mean of each group's set of numbers on the chalkboard before students complete item number 3.

Sugar Stack-Up

Purpose: To interpret a bar graph

Students will do the following:

- interpret data on a given bar graph
- answer questions related to given data

Materials for each student:

- copy of page 92
- pencil

Vocabulary to review:

- bar graph
- title
- axis

Extension activities to use after the reproducible:

- Help your class take note of the parts of a bar graph. Give each student a sticky note. Direct each student to write the name of her favorite candy on the note. Guide students in displaying the notes on the chalkboard, stacking each note by choice of candy. Then, as a class, make a bar graph using the data on the chalkboard, including a title and labeled axes.

- Follow up the above activity by having students create interpretive questions about the class bar graph. Ask students one or two questions about the information on the graph, such as how many different candies are represented on the graph or how many more students prefer one type of candy over another. Then pair students and direct each pair to write four or five questions that can be answered by interpreting the bar graph. Have pairs exchange papers with one another and use the graph to answer the questions. Afterward, have student volunteers share the questions and their answers.

Sugar Stack-Up

So just how much sugar is in your favorite candies? Use the bar graph at the right to see how these sugary snacks stack up against one another! Then complete the items that follow.

1. Which has less sugar, Starburst® or Twizzlers®? _____

2. Which has more sugar, M&M's® or Snickers®? _____

3. How much more sugar is contained in a Snickers than in a Reese's®? _____

4. Write the grams of sugar contained in each candy listed on the graph.

   M&M's _____   Snickers _____

   Reese's _____   Starburst _____

   _____ Twizzlers

5. If you ate one of each kind of candy, how many total grams of sugar would you be consuming? _____

6. Order the candies from the least to the greatest grams of sugar.

   _____

   _____

Bonus Box: On the back of this sheet, calculate the average amount of sugar found in the candies listed on the graph. **Hint:** To find an average, first add to find the total. Then divide the total by the number of items.

Sugar Found in Popular Candies

Grams of Sugar (g)

| | 0 | 2 | 4 | 6 | 8 | 10 | 12 | 14 | 16 | 18 | 20 | 22 | 24 | 26 | 28 | 30 | 32 |

Twizzlers® candy

Starburst® fruit chews

Snickers® bar

Reese's® peanut butter cups

M&M's® candy

Candy Names

Roll Into Bar Graphs!

Roll your students right into constructing bar graphs!

Purpose: To construct a bar graph

Students will do the following:

- collect and record data
- complete a frequency table
- construct a bar graph

Materials for each student:

- copy of page 94
- pencil
- pair of dice or 2 copies of the cube pattern on page 166 (numbered 1–6)
- scissors
- glue or tape

Vocabulary to review:

- bar graph
- frequency table

Extension activities to use after the reproducible:

- Help students make the grade in graphing with the following activity. Select one subject area, such as spelling, and have each student record his test grades in a notebook for one grading period. At the end of the grading period, have the student design a bar graph to display his results. Finally, have each student use the data to find the mean, median, and mode of his test scores.

- Use the graphing topics listed below in the following cooperative activity. Direct each group to choose a topic and conduct a class survey on it. Have the group collect its data in the form of a frequency table. Then have the group use the data to create a bar graph.

  — number of books read in a month
  — number of different cities visited
  — favorite season
  — favorite sport

  — type of shirts students are wearing (sleeve-less, short-sleeved, long-sleeved, button-down, pullover, etc.)
  — number of siblings

Name _____

Roll Into Bar Graphs!

Directions: Roll a pair of dice 50 times, recording the sum of each roll in the frequency table below. Then use the directions below to make a bar graph showing the results.

Frequency Table

Sum	2	3	4	5	6	7	8	9	10	11	12
Frequency											

To Construct a Bar Graph:

1. Label the grid's horizontal axis and vertical axis.
2. Determine a scale showing the number of rolls. (Choose a scale with an appropriate interval. Be sure all of your bars will fit on the graph provided.)
3. Look at the data on the frequency table. Construct a different bar for each sum.
4. Write a title for your graph.

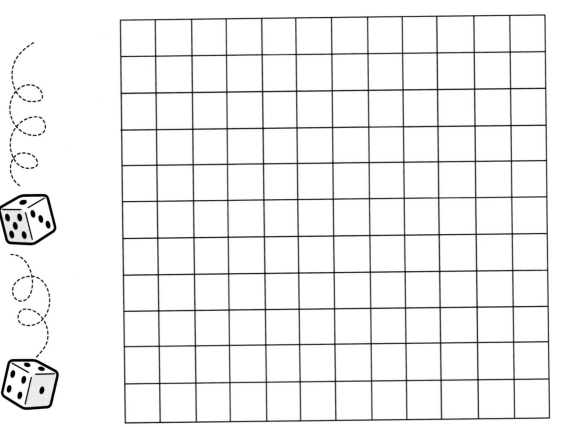

Bonus Box: Roll a pair of dice 20 times, recording the product of each roll in a frequency table on the back of this page. Create a bar graph to display your data.

©2001 The Education Center, Inc. • *Math Skills Workout* • TEC3229

Pedaling Pictographs

Put a new spin on interpreting pictographs with the following lesson.

Purpose: To interpret a pictograph

Students will do the following:

- interpret data presented in a pictograph
- answer questions related to data
- write number sentences

Materials for each student:

- copy of page 96
- pencil

Vocabulary to review:

- pictograph
- number sentence

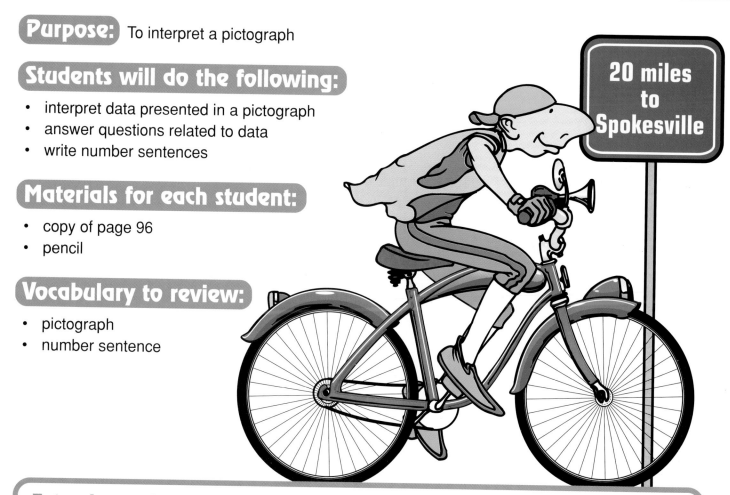

Extension activities to use after the reproducible:

- Write the problem shown below on the chalkboard. Then challenge each student to make a pictograph that displays the data in the problem. Direct the student to include a title, appropriate labeling, and a key for his graph.

  Mr. T. N. Speed owns four bicycle shops in four different cities. Last month he sold 130 bicycles at Pedaltown, 85 bicycles at Chainyville, 205 bicycles at Spin City, and 144 bicycles at his Spokesville shop. Create a pictograph to display the number of bicycles sold at each of Mr. T. N. Speed's shops last month.

- Use the charm of a popular cereal to improve students' graphing skills. Divide the class into groups of three. Give each group one cup of Lucky Charms® cereal. Have each group count the number of each marshmallow shape in its cup. Then write the totals from each group on the board (see the sample illustration at the right). After choosing a marshmallow shape as its symbol, direct each group to create a pictograph displaying the class totals for its shape.

Marshmallow Shape	Group Totals						Class Totals
	1	2	3	4	5	6	
Heart	10	3	5	12	6	8	44
Moon	14	8	6	9	10	4	51
Rainbow	8	12	9	4	2	6	41
Clover	11	13	3	7	5	9	48

Pedaling Pictographs

Business is booming at the Beachside Bicycle Shop. T. N. Speed, owner of the shop, uses pictographs to help him keep track of bicycle rentals. Use the graph below to answer the questions about last week's business.

Beachside Bicycle Shop Rentals

Key: ⚲ = 20 bicycle rentals

Day of the Week	Number of Rentals
Sunday	⚲ ⚲ ⚲ ⚲ ⚲ ⚲ ⚲ ⚲
Monday	⚲ ⚲ ⚲ ⚲ ⟠
Tuesday	⚲ ⚲ ⚲
Wednesday	⚲ ⚲ ⚲ ⚲ ⚲ ⟠
Thursday	⚲ ⚲ ⚲ ⚲ ⚲ ⚲ ⚲ ⟠
Friday	⚲ ⚲ ⚲ ⚲ ⚲ ⚲ ⚲ ⚲ ⚲ ⚲ ⚲
Saturday	⚲ ⚲ ⚲ ⚲ ⚲ ⚲ ⚲ ⚲ ⚲ ⚲ ⟠

Bonus Box: Calculate the number of rentals for each day of the week if ⚲ = 10 bicycle rentals.

1. How many bicycles were rented on Tuesday? _____

2. On what day did T. N. Speed rent 150 bicycles? _____

3. How many more bikes were rented on Thursday than on Tuesday? _____

4. Write a number sentence to show how many more bicycles were rented on Friday than on Sunday.

5. Is the total number of rentals on Tuesday and Wednesday more or less than the total number of rentals on Saturday?

6. If one bicycle rental costs $10, how much money did T. N. make on Saturday? _____

7. T. N.'s goal is to rent 1,200 bicycles each week. Did he meet his goal this week? Why or why not? _____

8. Write a number sentence to show the total number of bicycles rented on Friday, Saturday, and Sunday.

9. T. N. rented twice as many bicycles on Sunday than he did on _____

10. What was the average number of bicycles rented each day? (Round your answer to the nearest whole number.)

Coordinating Characters

Tell a tale of success after completing this coordinate graphing activity!

Purpose: To use ordered pairs to identify points on a grid

Students will do the following:

- identify letters given to ordered pairs
- write ordered pairs of numbers to spell words

Materials for each student:

- copy of page 98
- pencil

Vocabulary to review:

- coordinates
- ordered pair
- plot

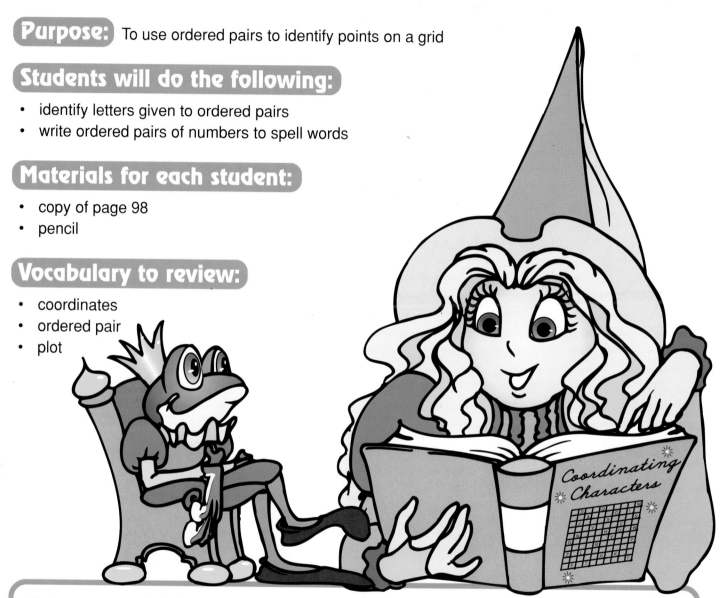

Extension activities to use after the reproducible:

- Continue the practice of plotting points with this simple partner activity. Give each student a copy of the 10 x 10 grid on page 165. Have each student plot all the letters of the alphabet on his grid. Pair students and then instruct one student in each pair to write a secret message to his partner, replacing each letter with an ordered pair. Direct the partner to use the coordinates to decode the message. As a variation, allow students to use the grids to practice spelling and vocabulary words.

- Challenge students to create symmetrical designs by plotting points on grids. Provide each student with two sheets of one-inch graph paper. Have the student number the horizontal and vertical axes of each sheet. Next, direct her to draw a symmetrical design on one of the grids. On another sheet of paper, have the student record the coordinate pairs necessary to make the design. Then have the student give the blank coordinate sheet along with the list of coordinates to a classmate to complete.

Coordinating Characters

Get reacquainted with these well-known folk and fairy-tale characters while practicing your coordinate-graphing skills. To discover the names of the characters, write the letter for each ordered pair in the blanks below. The first one has been started for you.

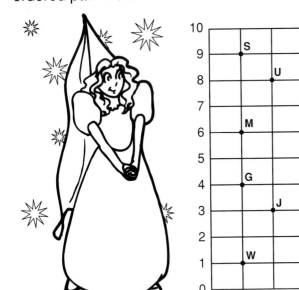
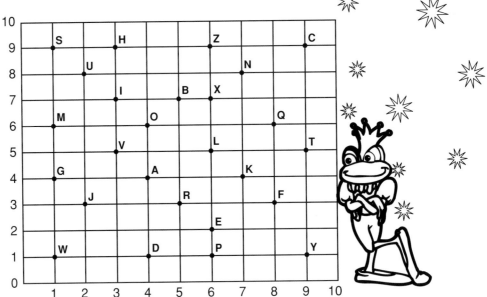

1. I won a race with a steam drill but died from fatigue at the moment of my victory.

   $\underset{(2,3)}{J}\ \underset{(4,6)}{\_\_}\ \underset{(3,9)}{\_\_}\ \underset{(7,8)}{\_\_}$ $\underset{(3,9)}{H}\ \underset{(6,2)}{\_\_}\ \underset{(7,8)}{\_\_}\ \underset{(5,3)}{\_\_}\ \underset{(9,1)}{\_\_}$

2. As a reward for being generous and honest, a fairy turned me into a real boy.

   ___ ___ ___ ___ ___ ___ ___ ___ ___
   (6, 1)(3, 7)(7, 8)(4, 6)(9, 9)(9, 9)(3, 9)(3, 7)(4, 6)

3. I retrieved the Princess's golden ball from the spring.

   ___ ___ ___ ___   ___ ___ ___ ___ ___ ___
   (8, 3)(5, 3)(4, 6)(1, 4)   (6, 1)(5, 3)(3, 7)(7, 8)(9, 9)(6, 2)

4. My stepmother tried to destroy me because of her jealousy.

   ___ ___ ___ ___   ___ ___ ___ ___ ___
   (1, 9)(7, 8)(4, 6)(1, 1)   (1, 1)(3, 9)(3, 7)(9, 5)(6, 2)

5. I am a Plains Indian trickster who is usually up to no good.

   ___ ___ ___ ___ ___ ___
   (3, 7)(7, 4)(9, 5)(4, 6)(1, 6)(3, 7)

6. According to legend, I taught broncos how to buck.

   ___ ___ ___ ___ ___   ___ ___ ___ ___
   (6, 1)(6, 2)(9, 9)(4, 6)(1, 9)   (5, 7)(3, 7)(6, 5)(6, 5)

7. Slaves enjoyed telling West African folk tales about me, a sly spider.

   ___ ___ ___ ___ ___ ___
   (4, 4)(7, 8)(4, 4)(7, 8)(1, 9)(3, 7)

8. I was given to the wicked witch at birth because my father was caught stealing from her garden.

   ___ ___ ___ ___ ___ ___ ___ ___
   (5, 3)(4, 4)(6, 1)(2, 8)(7, 8)(6, 9)(6, 2)(6, 5)

Bonus Box: Use the above grid to write the ordered pairs for the following character names: Cinderella, Goldilocks, Aladdin, and Hansel & Gretel.

The Bottom Line

Leapin' lizards! Show your students just how much fun line graphs can be!

Purpose: To interpret a line graph

Students will do the following:

- interpret data on a given line graph
- compare data on two graphs
- answer questions using given data
- find averages

Materials for each student:

- copy of page 100
- pencil

Vocabulary to review:

- line graph
- average

Extension activities to use after the reproducible:

- "Grow" your students' graphing skills with the following activity. Draw the line graph shown at the bottom left on a chalkboard or a transparency. Then have each student interpret the graph by answering the following four questions on loose-leaf paper:
  1. In which week did the marigolds grow the most? *(week 5)*
  2. In which week did the marigolds grow the least? *(week 1)*
  3. What was the average amount of growth over the five-week period? *(4 cm)*
  4. How many more centimeters did the marigolds grow in week 4 than in week 1? *(2 cm)*

- Continue keeping students tuned in to graphing with this practice activity. Draw the line graph shown at the bottom right on a chalkboard or a transparency. Direct each student to write four questions that can be answered using the data on the graph. Then have each student exchange papers with a partner and answer one another's questions.

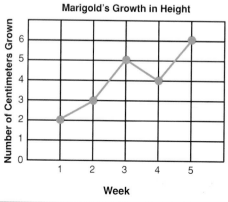

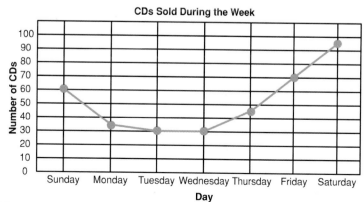

The Bottom Line

Keeping track of tickets at Reptile Park is no easy task! So Lizzy Lizard keeps graphs to help her get to "the bottom line" (the final number of ticket sales). Look at Lizzy's line graphs below. Then answer the questions that follow.

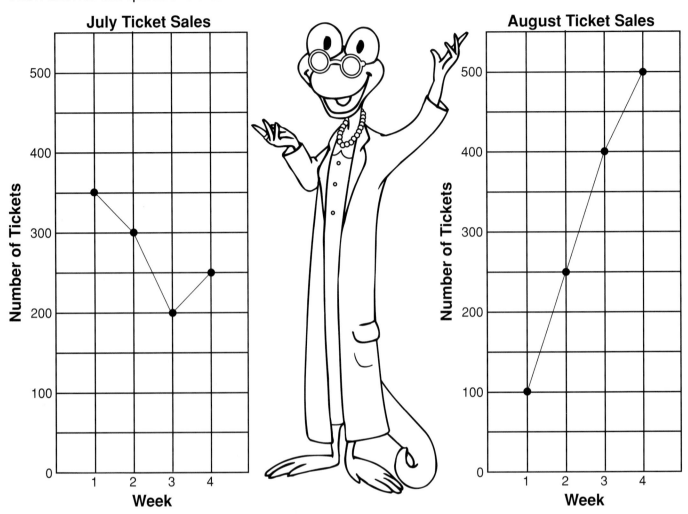

1. During which week in July were the most tickets sold? _____

2. During which week in August were the fewest tickets sold? _____

3. During which week in August were 400 tickets sold? _____

4. In which month did Reptile Park have a steady increase in ticket sales? _____

5. Identify the month and week that had the most ticket sales. _____

6. Calculate the average number of ticket sales in July. _____

7. Between which 2 weeks did July see the largest decrease in the number of tickets sold?
   _____ How much was the decrease? _____

8. For how many weeks in August were the sales over 200? _____

9. How many tickets were sold during week 2 in July? _____

10. Calculate the average number of ticket sales in August. (Round to the nearest whole number.) _____

Bonus Box: What might be the reason for the steady increase of ticket sales in August?

Lining Up a Great Season!

Shoot for success with this line-graphing activity!

Purpose: To construct a double line graph

Students will do the following:

- display data on a double line graph
- interpret data presented on a double line graph
- find averages

Materials for each student:

- copy of page 102
- pencil
- colored pencils or crayons

Vocabulary to review:

- double line graph
- average

Extension activities to use after the reproducible:

- Provide students with some poppin' good line-graphing practice! Display the following data on popcorn sales in a chart on the board. Then have each student use the data to create a line graph. Remind each student to label both axes and title her graph.

Popcorn Sales at the Goal City Stadium	
Game 1	450 bags
Game 2	300 bags
Game 3	225 bags
Game 4	625 bags
Game 5	500 bags

- Milk it for all it's worth! (Line-graphing practice, that is.) As a class, keep a record of how many students drink plain milk and how many students drink chocolate milk each day for one week. Display the data in a chart on a chalkboard or transparency. Then have each student construct a double line graph showing the daily number of plain-milk drinkers and chocolate-milk drinkers for the week. Finally, have each student write three sentences explaining the results of the graph.

Lining Up a Great Season!

What a year for basketball! The play was exciting and the fans were fabulous. Look at the scores for the first 5 games of the Gators vs. the Dragons. Use this information to make a double line graph comparing the scores. Use a different color to record each team's data. Then answer the questions that follow.

Goal City Gators	
Game	Points Scored
1	80
2	95
3	75
4	100
5	90

Dribbleville Dragons	
Game	Points Scored
1	55
2	90
3	85
4	80
5	95

Color Key

Gators   =

Dragons =

Gators vs. Dragons

[Graph grid with y-axis labeled "Points Scored" (50, 60, 70, 80, 90, 100) and x-axis labeled "Game" (1, 2, 3, 4, 5)]

1. Which team has won more games so far this season? _____

2. Who won Game 3 and by how many points? _____

3. What is the average score for the Dragons? _____

4. What is the average score for the Gators? _____

5. How many games have the Dragons won? _____

6. During which game did the Gators score 100 points? _____

7. During Game 2, how many more points did the Gators score than the Dragons? _____

8. During which game was the lowest number of points scored? _____

Bonus Box: Choose 1 of the teams from above and construct a pictograph to display its scores for each of the 5 games.

A Trip to the Mall

Spend time teaching students about circle graphs with this tantalizing trip to the mall!

Purpose: To interpret a circle graph

Students will do the following:

- interpret data on a given circle graph
- answer questions about circle graph data
- change percents to decimals
- multiply numbers with decimals

Materials for each student:

- copy of page 104
- pencil

Vocabulary to review:

- circle graph

Extension activities to use after the reproducible:

- Ready, set, time for more circle graph practice! Copy the data at the right onto the chalkboard or a transparency. Direct each student to construct a circle graph showing the number of hours spent in each store during a shopping spree. Remind the student to label each section of his circle with the name of the store from the list.

Hours Spent on a Shopping Spree (Total hours = 12 hours)	
Classy Clothing Store	4 hours
Awesome Arcade	1 hour
CD Warehouse	3 hours
Games Galore	1 hour
The Candy Bucket	1 hour
Sonic Electronics	2 hours

- Get students learning more about circle graphs with this cool activity. Copy the graph at the right onto the chalkboard or a transparency (omitting the italicized answers). Tell students that 20 people visited the ice-cream shop in the mall. Explain that the circle graph shows the percentage of people who chose each flavor of ice cream. Direct students to calculate the number of people represented on each section of the graph. Then have students write at least three sentences explaining the data shown on the graph.

vanilla
30%
(6 people)

chocolate
50%
(10 people)

strawberry
20%
(4 people)

A Trip to the Mall

Regina Richie really loves to spend money! Last week she spent her entire allowance of $80.00 while shopping at the mall. The circle graph below shows the percentage of money she spent at each store. Use the information in the graph to answer the questions that follow. **Hint:** Use the example below to help you figure a dollar amount using a percentage.

Example

$15\% = .15 \longrightarrow .15 \times \$80.00 = \$12.00$

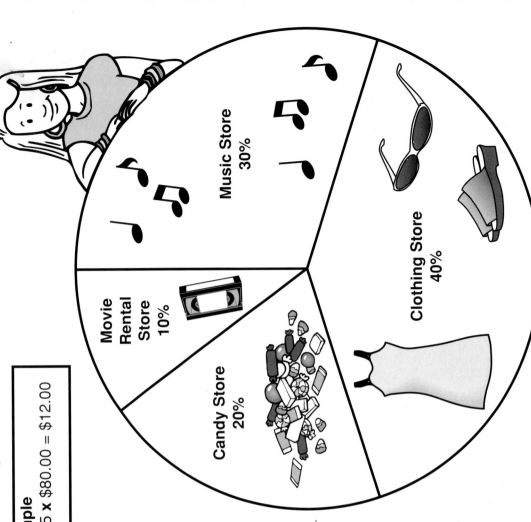

Music Store
30%

Movie Rental Store
10%

Candy Store
20%

Clothing Store
40%

1. In which store did Regina spend the most money? How much money did she spend? _____

2. In which store did Regina spend the least money? How much money did she spend? _____

3. How much more did Regina spend on clothes than on candy? _____

4. What percentage of money did Regina spend on music and clothes together? _____

5. How much more money did Regina spend on music than on movie rentals? _____

6. What if Regina spent $120.00 at the mall? Based on the same percentages, calculate the amounts she would spend on each of the following: music, clothes, candy, movies. _____

Bonus Box: Survey 10 classmates to find their favorite types of stores. Then, on the back of this page or on another sheet of paper, make a circle graph displaying the data.

Rounding Up Potato Favorites

Help your students grow to become best "spuds" with circle graphs!

Purpose: To construct and interpret a circle graph

Students will do the following:

- interpret a frequency table
- transfer data from a frequency table
- change fractions to percentages
- construct a circle graph

Materials for each student:

- copy of page 106
- pencil

Vocabulary to review:

- circle graph
- calculate
- percentage

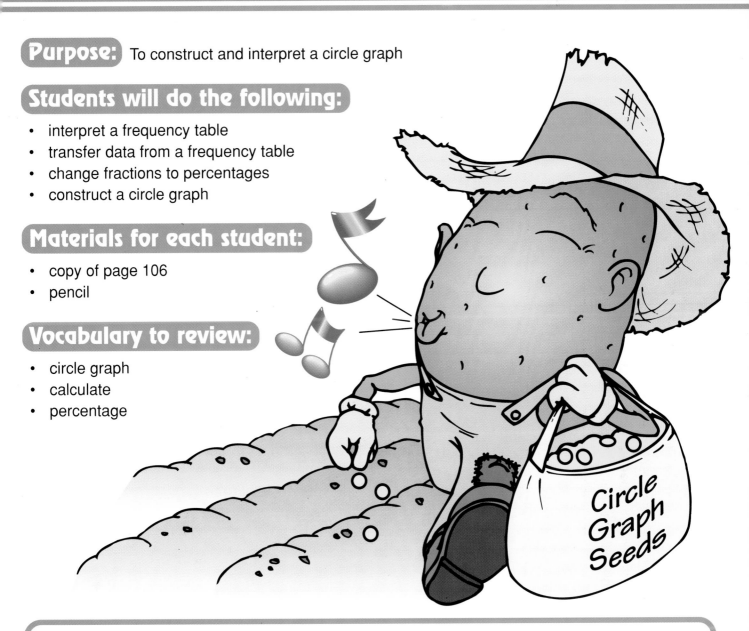

Extension activities to use after the reproducible:

- Find out if your students eat breakfasts fit for champions! Choose several breakfast foods, such as pancakes, eggs and bacon, cereal, and Pop-Tarts® toaster pastries. Survey your students to see which food they most often eat for breakfast. Record their responses on a chalkboard or transparency, making a tally mark for repetitive answers. As a class, calculate the percentage of students eating each breakfast food. Then have each student make a circle graph displaying the results.

- Get around to finding out what your students' favorites are. Divide students into groups of five. Give each group a different "favorites" topic, such as snacks, musical groups, TV shows, games, and sports. Next, direct each group to record each member's favorite as a fraction and then calculate a percentage for each one. Instruct each group to display its results on a circle graph. Finally, have groups share their favorites findings.

Rounding Up Potato Favorites

S. Pudlover, president of The Perfect Potato Company, polled 50 students to find out which type of potatoes they preferred. He constructed a frequency table displaying the results of his survey. Use the table to complete the following activities.

A. In the chart below, calculate the percentage of students who chose each type of potato. The first one has been done for you.

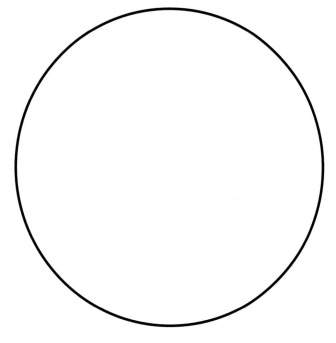

Potato	Frequency	Fraction	Percentage
mashed	20	$\dfrac{20}{50} = \dfrac{40}{100}$	40%
baked			
fried			
chips			

Potato Favorites

mashed	₶₶ ₶₶ ₶₶ ₶₶
baked	₶₶
fried	₶₶ ₶₶ ₶₶
chips	₶₶ ₶₶ ₶₶ ₶₶

B. Construct a circle graph using the data from your chart. Draw your graph using the circle below.

C. Write a memo to The Perfect Potato Company explaining the results shown in your circle graph.

On Course With Stem and Leaf Graphs

Help your students see the "hole" picture on constructing stem and leaf graphs.

Purpose: To interpret and construct stem and leaf graphs

Students will do the following:

- study steps in constructing a stem and leaf graph
- construct a stem and leaf graph using data given
- interpret the constructed stem and leaf graph

Materials for each student:

- copy of page 108
- pencil

Vocabulary to review:

- stem
- leaf/leaves
- data
- mean, median, mode, and range

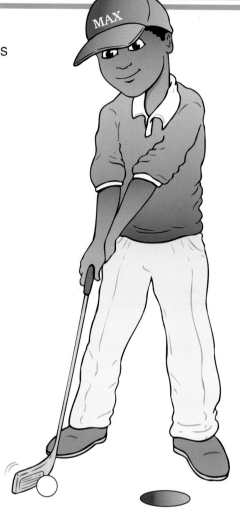

Extension activities to use after the reproducible:

- Help your students stand tall when it comes to constructing stem and leaf graphs! Direct pairs of students to use a yardstick or measuring tape to measure one another's height in inches and then report this data to you. Record the data on a chalkboard or a transparency. As a class, construct a stem and leaf graph displaying the heights of the students in your class. Then have pairs work together to find the mean, median, mode, and range of the data.

- Your students will give a winning score to this stem and leaf graphing activity! Copy the data shown below onto a chalkboard or a transparency. Divide students into groups and have each group display the data in a stem and leaf graph. Then direct groups to exchange papers and each write three facts that could be interpreted by using the given stem and leaf graph, such as "All the teams won between 17 and 62 games," and "The average number of games won was 41."

Games Won by Professional Basketball Teams During the 1994–1995 Season

57 55 35 32 30 24 21 52 50 47 43 42 34 28
62 60 47 41 36 21 59 57 48 44 39 26 17

On Course With Stem and Leaf Graphs

Max's Miniature Golf just celebrated its grand opening! In honor of the opening, Max held special teen tournaments throughout the month. Help Max organize information about the tournaments by completing the items below.

A. Study the steps below that explain how Max constructed a stem and leaf graph showing the number of teens who visited his golf course each day.

1. Max wrote the number of teens who visited each day in order from least to greatest.
   25 29 33 33 42 45 45 47 51 55 57 61 68 77 80 83 85 88 88 88

2. Max chose stem values. He used increments of 10 to represent the least to greatest values.

3. Max separated each number into stems (tens) and leaves (ones) in order from least to greatest.

4. Max titled the graph and wrote a key to explain how to read the stems and leaves.

Number of Teens Who Visited the Golf Course Each Day

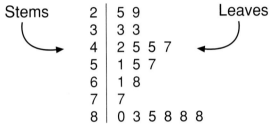

Stems		Leaves
2	5 9	
3	3 3	
4	2 5 5 7	
5	1 5 7	
6	1 8	
7	7	
8	0 3 5 8 8 8	

Key: 2 / 5 represents 25 visitors

B. Use the data listed below to construct a stem and leaf graph showing the teen tournament scores. Follow the steps above to help you construct your graph. Then answer the questions that follow.

Teen Tournament Scores

46 37 28 65 51 33 68 40 48 49 54 51 60 54 58 55 23 36 51 22 79

1. What was the mean score (average)? _____

2. What was the median score (the middle number when the set of numbers is ordered from least to greatest)? _____

3. Which score occurred most often (mode)? _____

4. What was the range of scores (the difference between the greatest and least numbers)?

_____

Bonus Box: Use Max's chart to find the mean, median, mode, and range of the number of teens who visited his golf course each day. Write your answers on the back of this sheet.

Note to the teacher: Explain to students that to find the median of an even set of numbers, find the average of the 2 middle numbers.

The School of Graphing

Hook your students on different types of graphs with this "reel-ly" exciting activity!

Purpose: To match appropriate graphs with given data

Students will do the following:

- analyze given graphs
- match each graph with its appropriate data
- write to explain their answers

Materials for each student:

- copy of page 110
- pencil

Vocabulary to review:

- bar graph
- line graph
- pictograph
- circle graph
- data

Extension activities to use after the reproducible:

- Reinforce the skill of selecting an appropriate graph through this group activity. Divide students into groups of four. Assign each group a different type of graph. Direct the group to create data for an imaginary school-related function, such as the number of tickets sold for a sports event, that can be displayed in its assigned graph. After each group completes its graph, have the group explain why its graph is an appropriate display for the data.

- Generate some great graphing practice with this newsworthy activity. Gather examples of various types of graphs from a newspaper, such as *USA Today*®. Divide students into groups of four. Then give each group several different graphs, construction paper, glue, and a marker. Have the group glue each graph to a separate sheet of construction paper. At the top of the construction paper, have the group title the graph appropriately. Next, direct the group to write a paragraph on the back of the paper summarizing the data presented in the graph. Finally, bind the sheets together into a class book titled "A Great Book of Graphs."

Comparing graphs

The School of Graphing

Directions: Below are 8 situations in which the given data could be displayed on a graph. Read each situation carefully; then match it with the correct graph. Write the matching letter below the graph, and then explain your answer. Use the back of this page if you need more space to write.

A. The temperature steadily increased throughout the school day.

B. Pizza sales started out high, but slowly declined over the first month of the fund-raiser.

C. The teacher handed out an equal amount of each color of construction paper.

D. The school collected pounds of recyclable materials for paper, plastic, and aluminum.

E. More than half the students surveyed chose free time as their weekly reward.

F. Fifteen students chose South America as the continent they'd like to visit most.

G. Twice as many students chose hamburgers than chose hot dogs as their favorite picnic food.

H. Basketball and soccer received an equal amount of votes as a favorite sport.

4. Situation: _____
   Explain: _____

8. Situation: _____
   Explain: _____

3. Situation: _____
   Explain: _____

7. Situation: _____
   Explain: _____

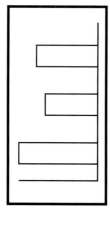

2. Situation: _____
   Explain: _____

6. Situation: _____
   Explain: _____

1. Situation: _____
   Explain: _____

5. Situation: _____
   Explain: _____

Bonus Box: Choose 1 of the above situations and matching graphs. On the back of this sheet, complete the graph using imaginary data. Be sure to appropriately label the graph.

Playing Around With Properties

Help your students win at identifying and using the properties of multiplication!

Purpose: To identify and use the properties of multiplication

Students will do the following:

- play a game to identify and use the properties of multiplication

Materials for each group of four players:

- copy of page 112
- copy of answer key on page 173
- 3 different-colored game pieces
- die
- sheet of paper
- pencil

Vocabulary to review:

- distributive property
- commutative property
- associative property
- property of one
- zero property
- variable

Distributive Property—Write a
factor as the sum of addends.
Then multiply each addend by
the other factor.
2 x 57 = (2 x 50) + (2 x 7) = 100 + 14 = 114
Commutative Property—Multiply
the factors in any order.
4 x 2 = 2 x 4 = 8
Associative Property—Group the factors
in any way.
(4 x 5) x 3 = 4 x (5 x 3) = 60
Property of One—Multiplying a factor
and 1 results in the product being
the factor.
38 x 1 = 38
Zero Property—Multiplying a factor and
0 results in the product being 0.
77 x 0 = 0

24 = 24 x 1
5 x 1 = 5

Property
of One

Extension activities to use after the reproducible:

- Have students put their heads together to show that four heads are better than one when it comes to identifying the properties of multiplication. In advance, label sheets of construction paper with two examples of each property above, writing the examples on the front, the property on the back. Divide students into groups of four. Assign each group a different number and each group member a different number from one to four. Hold up one example at a time and challenge group members to put their heads together to identify the property. Then call out a specific group and a number from one to four. Allow the student having that number to confer with his group members before answering. After the correct property has been identified, continue with the next card.

- Focus on the distributive property with this assessment activity. Write the problems below on the board (without the answers). Have students use the distributive property to solve the problems. Check the answers together. Then direct each child to write a paragraph explaining how the distributive property helped her solve one of the problems.

  1. 59 x 3
     (50 x 3) + (9 x 3) = 150 + 27 = 177
  2. 753 x 5
     (700 x 5) + (50 x 5) + (3 x 5) = 3,500 + 250 + 15 = 3,765
  3. 4,251 x 2
     (4,000 x 2) + (200 x 2) + (50 x 2) + (1 x 2) = 8,000 + 400 + 100 + 2 = 8,502

Playing Around With Properties

Use what you know about the properties of multiplication to be the game's high scorer!

Number of Players: 4

Materials: gameboard, game piece for each player, die, answer key, sheet of paper

Directions: Place the game pieces on Start. Select a player to sit out of the game and be the scorekeeper. Give this player the answer key. Player 1 rolls the die, moves his game piece that number of spaces, and completes the task for that space (either identifying the property or both identifying the property and solving the problem on paper). If correct, he earns the assigned number of points on the space. If incorrect, he earns no points. Continue play in this manner, with each player taking turns. When all players reach Finish, declare the player with the most points the winner—and the scorekeeper of the next game.

Properties of Multiplication
Zero Property: $0 \times y = 0$
Property of One: $1 \times y = y$
Commutative Property: $a \times b = b \times a$
Associative Property: $a \times (b \times c) = (a \times b) \times c$
Distributive Property: $365 \times y = (300 \times y) + (60 \times y) + (5 \times y) = 300y + 60y + 5y = 365y$

| **START** | Identify (1 point)

$12 \times 1 = 12$

① | Identify (1 point)

$6 \times 4 = 4 \times 6$

② | Identify (1 point)
Solve (2 points)

$362 \times 1 = $ _____
③ | Identify (1 point)

$0 \times 5 = 0$

④ |

Identify (1 point)
$67 \times 2 = (60 \times 2) + (7 \times 2) = 120 + 14 = 134$
⑤

| Identify (1 point)
Solve (2 points)
$12 \times 4 = $ ____ $\times$ ____ = _____
⑩ | Identify (1 point)
Solve (2 points)

$10 \times 0 = $ _____
⑨ | Identify (1 point)

$7 \times (2 \times 4) = (7 \times 2) \times 4$
⑧ | Identify (1 point)
Solve (2 points)

$17 \times 1 = $ _____
⑦ | Identify (1 point)
Solve (2 points)
$2 \times (3 \times 4) = ($ ___ $\times$ ___ $)$ $\times$ ___ = ___ $\times$ ___ = ____
⑥ |

Identify (1 point)
Solve (2 points)

$19 \times 0 = $ _____
⑪

| Identify (1 point)
Solve (2 points)

$63 \times 4 = $ ____ $\times$ ____ = _____
⑫ | Identify (1 point)

$(7 \times 8) \times 9 = 7 \times (8 \times 9)$

⑬ | Identify (1 point)

$741 \times 8 = (700 \times 8) + (40 \times 8) + (1 \times 8) = 5,600 + 320 + 8 = 5,928$
⑭ | Identify (1 point)
Solve (2 points)
$58 \times 9 = ($ _____ $) + ($ _____ $) = $ _____ $+$ _____ = _____
⑮ | **FINISH** |

The Ins and Outs of Function Tables

Help your students successfully maneuver the ins and outs
of function tables!

Purpose: To complete function tables containing variables

Students will do the following:

- identify the rule for a function table
- complete a function table by applying the rule

Materials for each student:

- copy of page 114
- pencil

Vocabulary to review:

- variable
- rule
- input
- output
- algebraic expression

Extension activities to use after the reproducible:

- Strengthen students' understanding of how to complete function tables with this hands-on activity. Give each student 20 cubes and a math mat. Next, write the function table at the right (without the answers) on the board. Instruct the student to place 12 cubes on his mat. Next, have him follow the directions of the table's output column (to remove three cubes) and identify the first output number *(9)*. Continue in this manner until students determine the four remaining output numbers. Follow up by having students repeat the process with another function table, using the rule a + 5, when a = 8, 10, 12, 14, and 16.

y	y − 3
12	9
14	11
16	13
18	15
20	17

- Assess students' understanding of function tables by having them complete a two-part task. Write the function table at the right (without the answers) on the chalkboard. Direct each student to copy and complete the table on a sheet of paper. Then have each student add a paragraph explaining how he interpreted the rule for this table and identified the value of its five output numbers.

x	2x + 5
5	15
6	17
7	19
8	21
9	23

The Ins and Outs of Function Tables

Reggie the Robot is programmed to complete function tables that contain variables. Unfortunately, Reggie is experiencing a wiring glitch and will be unable to meet his deadline—unless you help him! Identify the value of the variable in each function table below. Then complete the table to identify the missing input or output number in each row.

1.

x	x − 15
50	___
60	___
70	___
80	___

2.

x	x ÷ 5
45	___
50	___
55	___
60	___

3.

x	4x
8	___
___	40
___	60
14	___

4.

x	8 + x
___	17
12	___
15	___
___	26

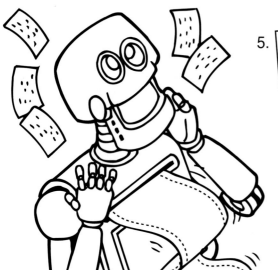

5.

x	x ÷ 7
21	___
___	4
35	___
___	7

6.

x	21 − x
5	___
10	___
___	6
___	1

7.

x	7x
5	___
8	___
___	77
___	105

8.

x	x + 13
5	___
7	___
___	24
___	30

Bonus Box: Replace the input column in Table 3 with the following numbers: 12, 15, 18, 24. Calculate the new output numbers.

In Step With Ordered Pairs

Help your students stay in step when practicing ordered pairs!

Purpose: To identify and use patterns in ordered pairs

Students will do the following:

- identify an equation that represents the pattern of a set of ordered pairs
- write an equation that represents the relation of a set of ordered pairs
- write a set of ordered pairs that represents a relation

Materials for each student:

- copy of page 116
- pencil

Vocabulary to review:

- ordered pair
- equation
- relation
- pattern
- algebraic expression

Extension activities to use after the reproducible:

- Help students become high steppers when it comes to identifying relations in ordered pairs. Copy each set of ordered pairs below (without the equations) on the chalkboard. Have students write the equation that represents each relation. Let x equal the first number in the pair and y equal the second number. Then challenge students to explain how they know their answers are correct.

  $y = x + 5$: (1, 6), (2, 7), (3, 8), (4, 9), (5, 10) $y = 3x$: (1, 3), (2, 6), (3, 9), (4, 12), (5, 15)

- Keep students in step with identifying patterns in ordered pairs with a file-folder activity that's perfect for a math center. Gather one file folder, seven library pocket cards, and six small index cards. Open the file folder; then glue five pockets to the right side of the folder, one to the left side, and one to the back side of the folder. Label each pocket on the right side of the folder with a different equation below. If desired, add a note at the top of the folder stating that x equals the first number in the pair and y equals the second number. Next, write each set of ordered pairs on a separate index card. Shuffle the five cards and place them in the pocket on the left side of the folder. Use the remaining index card for the answer key and place it in the pocket on the back of the folder. To use the center, direct students to remove the cards from the left pocket, identify the pattern of each set of ordered pairs, and then place the card in the matching pocket on the folder's right side.

Equation	Matching Set of Ordered Pairs
$y = x + 1$	(2, 3), (3, 4), (4, 5), (5, 6), (6, 7)
$x = y - 5$	(5, 10), (6, 11), (7, 12), (8, 13), (9, 14)
$x = y \div 3$	(2, 6), (3, 9), (4, 12), (5, 15), (6, 18)
$y = 4x$	(2, 8), (3, 12), (4, 16), (5, 20), (6, 24)
$y = x + 7$	(1, 8), (2, 9), (3, 10), (4, 11), (5, 12)

In Step With Ordered Pairs

How can you get in step—and stay in step—with ordered pairs? Just follow the directions in each section below!

Part I: Study the set of ordered pairs on each shoe print below. Identify the relation between the numbers in each pair. Then, on the matching shoe print, write an equation that represents the relation. Let x equal the first number in the pair and y equal the second number.

1.

(4, 5), (5, 6), (6, 7), (7, 8), (8, 9)

_____

2.

(4, 8), (5, 9), (6, 10), (7, 11), (8, 12)

_____

3.

(1, 5), (2, 10), (3, 15), (4, 20), (5, 25)

_____

4.

(5, 10), (6, 12), (7, 14), (8, 16), (9, 18)

_____

Part II: Use the equation written on each shoe print to help you write a set of 5 ordered pairs that represent it. Hint: x equals the first number in the pair and y equals the second number.

5.

$y = x + 2$

_____

6.

$x = y - 3$

_____

7.

$y = 2x$

_____

8.

$x = 10 - y$

_____

Bonus Box: Write your own set of 5 ordered pairs that can represent the equation $y = 2x + 3$.

Recipe for Graphing Ordered Pairs

Get students cooking with an activity that has the right ingredients for graphing ordered pairs!

Purpose: To graph ordered pairs

Students will do the following:

- identify the relation between x and y variables
- complete function tables to identify ordered pairs
- graph ordered pairs in one quadrant

Materials for each student:

- copy of page 118
- pencil

Vocabulary to review:

- ordered pairs
- relation
- variables
- function table

(3, 5)
(4, 6)
(5, 7)

Extension activities to use after the reproducible:

- Show students that graphing ordered pairs is in the cards with this extension activity. Display for students three sets of cards: Set One, three hearts and two clubs; Set Two, four hearts and two clubs; Set Three, five hearts and two clubs. Announce that y represents the total number of cards in each set and x represents the number of hearts. Guide students to identify the relation that represents the three sets of cards *(y = x + 2)*. Finally, challenge students to use the relation to complete the function table at the right and then graph the resulting ordered pairs.

x	y
3	
4	
5	
6	
7	

- Set up a math center to help students review function tables and the graphing of ordered pairs. Write each relation at the right and its corresponding values for x on a different index card. Place the cards at a center along with pencils and sheets of graphing paper. Direct each student using the center to take one card and complete the function table on the card on the back of the graph paper. Then have him graph the resulting ordered pairs on the front.

1. y = x − 2

x	y
15	
13	
11	
9	
7	

2. y = 3x

x	y
2	
3	
4	
5	
6	

3. y = x ÷ 3

x	y
15	
12	
9	
6	
3	

Recipe for Graphing Ordered Pairs

Yum! Grandma's making her famous pineapple-orange upside-down cake!
Now—while it's baking—is the perfect time to practice graphing ordered pairs.

Directions:

Each function table below represents the relation between a pair of ingredients in Grandma's cake recipe. Complete each table. Then use each table's ordered pairs to construct a line graph on the grid provided.

1. $y = x + 3$

   x = cups of sugar
   y = cups of flour

x	y
2	
3	
4	
5	
6	

2. $y = 2x$

   x = teaspoons of cinnamon
   y = teaspoons of vanilla

x	y
1	
3	
5	
7	
9	

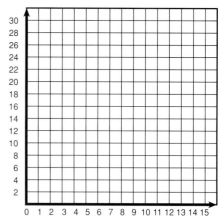

3. $y = x \div 2$

   x = ounces of milk
   y = ounces of butter

x	y
16	
20	
24	
28	
32	

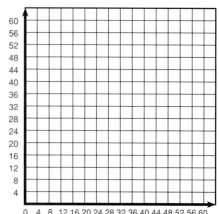

Bonus Box: Oops! Grandma just changed her recipe! The relation between flour and sugar is now $y = x + 5$. Create and complete a function table for the new ordered pairs on the back of this page. Then graph the pairs.

The Case of the Missing Digits

Have your students become sleuths to take the mystery out of finding unknown factors and addends!

Purpose: To find the value of a variable in an equation

Students will do the following:

- identify the unknown addend or factor when given the other numbers in an equation
- solve a riddle using unknown addends and factors

Materials for each student:

- copy of page 120
- loose-leaf paper
- pencil

Vocabulary to review:

- addend
- factor
- variable
- algebraic equation

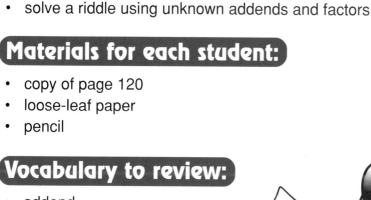

Extension activities to use after the reproducible:

- Solving for unknown addends won't be a mystery for long with this hands-on activity. Gather a bag of 30 counters or cubes for yourself. Give a similar bag to each pair of students. Write the equation $10 + x = 15$ on the board. Direct the pairs to use their counters to solve the equation along with you. Remove ten counters from your bag and place them on a desktop. Add counters until you have 15 counters. Announce that since five counters were added together, $x = 5$ because $10 + 5 = 15$. Next, write the equation $15 + n = 22$ on the board. Challenge students to use their counters to find the value of n. Check the answer together. Follow up by writing two more equations on the board (without the answers) for students to solve, such as $18 + n = 28$ *(n = 10)* and $21 + p = 25$ *(p = 4)*.

- Remove the mystery of finding the value of unknown factors by creating this card game for your math center. First, make a set of matching index cards, writing an equation with an unknown factor on one card, such as $r \times 6 = 30$, and the number representing the unknown factor (in this case, 5) on another. Then instruct students using the center to turn the cards facedown and take turns turning over two cards at a time until all the matches have been made.

The Case of the Missing Digits

Detective Wolfington's latest case involves finding unknown factors and addends. His only clues are the equations listed below. Find the value of the variable in each equation. Then write the letter on the hat next to each equation in its matching blank to answer the riddle.

1. $a + 12 = 17$ A
   a = _____

2. $168 \div k = 42$ K
   k = _____

3. $102 - s = 84$ S
   s = _____

4. $52 + t = 75$ T
   t = _____

5. $88 - a = 57$ A
   a = _____

6. $t \div 8 = 4$ T
   t = _____

7. $i \times 14 = 84$ I
   i = _____

8. $9 \times c = 99$ C
   c = _____

9. $t \div 9 = 7$ T
   t = _____

10. $s \times 4 = 32$ S
    s = _____

11. $u + 47 = 95$ U
    u = _____

12. $y - 33 = 33$ Y
    y = _____

13. $98 - o = 12$ O
    o = _____

14. $144 \div i = 12$ I
    i = _____

15. $12 \times n = 84$ N
    n= _____

16. $39 + i = 56$ I
    i = _____

What did Detective Wolfington call the Case of the Missing Bubble Gum?

___ ___ ___ ___ ___ ___ ___   ___ ___ ___ ___ ___ ___ ___ ___ ___
 5   8   23 12 11 4   66   18 6   63 48 31 32 17 86 7

Bonus Box: Select any 3 equations above. On the back of this page, write a story problem that could represent each equation.

The Language of Inequalities

Teach your students the art of using algebraic expressions to communicate inequalities!

Purpose: To write algebraic expressions that represent inequalities

Students will do the following:

- interpret written situations
- write an algebraic expression that represents a situation

Materials for each student:

- copy of page 122
- pencil

Vocabulary to review:

- inequality
- greater than
- less than
- variable
- algebraic expression

Extension activities to use after the reproducible:

- Present inequalities from a different perspective with this hands-on activity. In advance, write "< 10" on a paper lunch bag and fill it with nine centimeter cubes. Write "< 20" on a second bag, filling it with 19 cubes. Write "< 30" on a third bag, filling it with 21 cubes. Then follow the steps below.

  1. Display the < 10 bag for students. Write "$n < 10$" on the board. Explain that this expression represents the number of objects that could be in the bag. Ask students to name the range of all possible objects that could be in the bag *(0 to 9)*. Next, remove seven cubes from the bag; then write "$n - 7 < 10$" on the board. Explain to students that this expression represents the number of objects now in the bag.

  2. Display the < 20 bag. Ask students to name the range of all possible objects that could be in the bag *(0 to 19)*. Remove six cubes from the bag. Challenge students to write an expression that represents all the possible objects that could be in the bag *($n - 6 < 20$)*.

  3. Display the < 30 bag. Add eight cubes to it. Ask students to name the range of all possible objects that could be in the bag after the eight cubes were added to it *(8 to 37)*. Conclude by having students write an expression that represents this situation *($n + 8 < 38$)*.

- Assess students' understanding of inequalities by having them respond to the journal prompt below.

  Explain the expression $36 > x + 30$. Then list all the possible values of x. *($x < 6$)*

The Language of Inequalities

Shopping fever has hit the stores at Centerville's shopping mall this week because of a big sale. Use the variable *n* and an inequality symbol to write an expression that represents each situation below.

What a sale! Every pound of candy at Sweet Sue's Candy Shoppe is only $1.00!

Sweet Sue's Candy Shoppe
THIS WEEK ONLY!
All Candy $1.00 per Pound!
Chocolate Clusters!   Peanut Brittle!
All Flavors of Fudge!
Gumdrops!   Jelly Beans!

1. The preteen section of the department store never has more than 36 T-shirts to sell. Five T-shirts were sold on Monday.

   _____

2. T-shirts cost $7.00 each at Crazy T's. Jamie knows he must spend less than $49.00 on his purchases.

   _____

3. At Soccer Time, Curt and his teammates divided 24 pairs of soccer socks. Each player got no more than 6 pairs each.

   _____

4. Katie just sold 7 sweatshirts at Sweatshirts Galore. There were no more than 12 sweatshirts left to sell.

   _____

5. The cheerleaders at Centerville High have $28.00 to rent a bullhorn. A bullhorn at Loud Mike's rents for $4.00 an hour, plus a $7.00 deposit fee.

   _____

6. Fewer than 40 people can fit comfortably inside Mr. Z's CD Store at a time. There were 27 people already inside the store when some more customers entered.

   _____

7. Maggie has $25.00 to spend on sweatpants. Baggy Sweats, Inc., is out of sweatpants. To order the sweatpants, the cost will be $7.00 each, plus $3.00 shipping for the total order.

   _____

8. Teacher Appreciation Week is coming up, and Julie wants to buy mugs for her 9 teachers. She has saved $52.00.

   _____

Bonus Box: Look back at problem 6 above. On the back of this page, list all the possible sizes of the groups (of at least 2 customers) that could enter Mr. Z's CD Store. Then write a paragraph explaining how you got your answers.

An Equation Vacation!

Send students on an imaginary vacation that's perfect for writing equations!

Purpose: To write algebraic equations that represent situations

Students will do the following:

- interpret written situations
- write an algebraic equation that represents a situation

Materials for each student:

- copy of page 124
- pencil

Vocabulary to review:

- algebraic equation
- variable

Extension activities to use after the reproducible:

- For additional practice in writing algebraic equations, present students with three additional situations related to those on page 124. Copy the statements below (without the answers) onto the chalkboard. Have each student write an algebraic equation to represent each one. Then check the answers together.

  1. Vivian took 18 pictures with her camera. She has only six shots left. $(x - 18 = 6)$

  2. Van rented a bike for two hours and paid an extra $3 to rent a helmet. All together he spent $11. $(2x + 3 = 11)$

  3. Veronica won three stuffed animals to add to her collection. Now she has a total of 13 plush toys. $(x + 3 = 13)$

- Pull out base-ten blocks for a small-group, hands-on activity that reinforces the writing of algebraic equations. Divide students into groups of two or three. Give each group a set of base-ten blocks consisting of nine rods and nine units. Instruct each group to display three rods and four units on a desktop. Then write the equation $3x + 4 = 34$ on the board. Have students find the value of the variable *(10)*. Next, instruct students to display five rods and six units. Ask students to identify an algebraic equation that could represent the displayed blocks $(5x + 6 = 56)$. Finally, challenge each group to use its blocks to show and record two additional examples of algebraic equations to share with the class.

An Equation Vacation!

Vernon and Vivian Variable, along with their kids, Van, Velma, and Veronica, are on their annual beach vacation. Using x as the variable, write an algebraic equation to represent each situation below.

1.
Vivian tripled the number of seashells she collected. Now she has 51.

_____

2.
Veronica used 18 of her ride tickets. Now she has 14.

_____

3.

Van took 12 juice boxes to the beach to share equally among his friends. Each friend got 3 drink boxes.

_____

4.
Vernon added 2 more scoops of ice cream to the family's super sundae. Now the sundae has 15 scoops of ice cream.

_____

5.
Velma made a sand castle that had 24 towers. After a wave hit it, there were only 16 towers.

_____

6.
Vivian bought 4 rolls of film and used a coupon for $3.00 off her purchase. She spent $9.00.

_____

7.
Each boardwalk game Veronica played cost $2.00 each. She used $10.00 of her money on the games.

_____

8.
Van spent $5.00 playing miniature golf and bought 2 snow cones to cool off. He spent a total of $9.00.

_____

Bonus Box: Look back at problem 6. If Vivian's film had cost $5.00 a roll, how much money would she have spent?

The Positives and Negatives of the Fun Fair

Turn students' work with negative numbers into
opportunities for positive practice!

Purpose: To identify and use positive and negative numbers to represent a situation

Students will do the following:

- interpret written situations
- use a negative number to represent a situation
- use a positive number to represent a situation
- determine the opposite of a number

Materials for each student:

- copy of page 126
- pencil

Vocabulary to review:

- negative numbers
- positive numbers
- integers
- opposites

Extension activities to use after the reproducible:

- See how keen your students' understanding of negative numbers actually is with this cooperative writing activity. Divide students into groups of four. Give each group a sheet of chart paper and an index card labeled with a negative number. Challenge the group to write a realistic situation on the paper that is represented by its negative number. When students have finished writing, have each group pass its card to another group. Each group then writes another situation represented by the new card's negative number. Continue in this manner until every group has written a situation represented by each of the negative numbers. Then have each group share two of its situations with the class and have classmates guess the answers. If desired, also have the class provide the opposite for each negative number.

- Use a trusty visual aid to help students represent the positives and negatives of a situation. Display a number line or draw the one below on a chalkboard. Write the situation below on the board for students to read. Then challenge students to use the number line to move from number to number to identify the negative number that represents the situation.

Lane owed his brother $3. He earned $8 mowing lawns and paid his brother back. Next, he wanted to buy a new water bottle for $6. How much more money does he need? *($1)*

The Positives and Negatives of the Fun Fair

Math Town's Fun Fair has just opened for business! Use the illustration of the Powerful Plunge to solve each problem below.

Vocabulary

- Numbers greater than 0 are **positive numbers.**
- Numbers less than 0 are **negative numbers.**
- **Integers** include natural numbers (1, 2, 3…), their opposites, and 0.
- **Opposites** are 2 nonzero numbers the same distance from 0 on a number line; 1 number is positive and the other is negative.

1. If the Powerful Plunge begins at ground level and falls 40 feet and then rises 30 feet, what is its location? _____
   What is the opposite of this number?

   _____

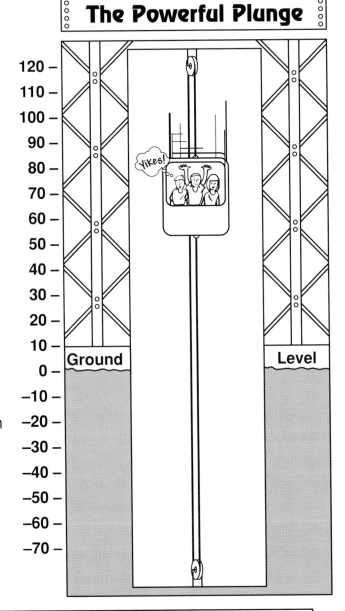

2. If the ride begins at –60 and then rises 100 feet, what is its location? _____

3. What is the distance between the lowest point (70 feet below ground level) and the highest point (120 feet above ground level) on the Powerful Plunge? _____

4. The ride stalled at 30 feet. What is the opposite of this number? _____

5. The Powerful Plunge is very unpredictable. You never know when the ride will stop climbing upward and begin its quick plunge downward. If the ride rises only 10 feet from ground level and then quickly plunges 60 feet, what is its location? _____

Bonus Box: On the back of this page, write 2 more problems about the Powerful Plunge. Include answers.

Back-Flip Problem Solving

Your students will flip over these working-backward problems!

Purpose: To solve problems using the working-backward strategy

Students will do the following:

- interpret clue words given
- calculate inverse operations
- add and subtract

Materials for each student:

- copy of page 128
- pencil

Vocabulary to review:

- four times
- twice as many
- half as many
- less than
- more than

Extension activities to use after the reproducible:

- Make working backward fun with these reverse riddles! Write the following number riddle on the board: "If you multiply my number by five, subtract three, and then divide by two, the result will be 11." *(The number is five.)* Below the problem, solve the riddle by using the inverse operation of every step. *(11 x 2 = 22; 22 + 3 = 25; 25 ÷ 5 = 5)* Then instruct each student to write a reverse riddle of her own and exchange it with a partner to solve.

- Combine writing with math when students write their own working-backward word problems. Write the following number sentence on the board: "_____ + 2 − 3 = 9." Then write the following word problem: "Susie wanted to know Ben's age. He told her that if she added two to his age and then subtracted three, she'd end up with nine. How old is Ben?" *(ten years old)* Next, give each student one index card. Using the problem on the board as an example, have each student write a similar word problem on the front of his index card and the answer on the back. Collect the cards then redistribute them for students to solve. *(Make sure that students do not receive their own cards.)*

Back-Flip Problem Solving

Stretch your mind and show off your math moves. Remember to flip back through the information in each problem to find the solution!

Directions: Read each problem below. Then work backward to solve the problem. Write the answer in the blank provided.

1. Four fifth-grade gymnasts have won individual events so far this year. Susie has won 4 times as many events as Laura. Chelsea has won 6 more events than Susie. Ben has won half as many events as Susie. Laura has won 4 events. How many events has Ben won so far?

   Answer: _____

2. Every week, the gym club members hold a bake sale. In week 4, they raised twice as much money as they did in week 3. In week 3, the club raised $8.75 less than in week 2. In week 2 the club raised $13.80 more than in week 1. In week 1 the club raised $23.10. How much did the club raise in week 4?

   Answer: _____

3. Lisa, Liz, Lindsey, and Larry competed against each other in the floor exercise. Liz did 3 times as many back flips as Larry. Larry did 2 more back flips than Lisa. Lisa did half as many back flips as Lindsey. Lindsey did 4 back flips. How many back flips did Liz do?

   Answer: _____

4. It is 6:00 P.M., and Jenna is still at practice. She has spent 45 minutes on the uneven bars, 40 minutes on the balance beam, 1 hour on her floor exercise, and 35 minutes practicing her vault. What time did she begin practicing?

   Answer: _____

5. The coach placed groups of gymnasts in different practice areas. She placed half the gymnasts at the vault and divided the remaining gymnasts equally among the balance beam, floor mats, and uneven bars. There were 15 gymnasts at the balance beam. How many gymnasts were at practice?

   Answer: _____

Bonus Box: On the back of this sheet, design a bar graph to display the number of back flips that each student performed in problem 3.

Making "Cents" out of Working Backward

Challenge your students to ring up solutions to these money-matters problems by using the working-backward strategy!

Purpose: To solve problems using the working-backward strategy

Students will do the following:

- interpret clues given in word problems
- use all four operations to solve money problems
- write to explain

Materials for each student:

- copy of page 130
- loose-leaf paper
- pencil
- calculator (optional)

Vocabulary to review:

- purchases
- twice as many/much
- three times as many
- half as many

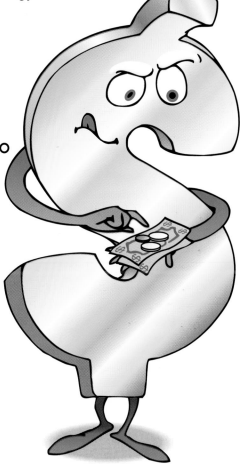

Hmmm...the total was $15. My change was $5. So I must have paid with a $20 bill.

Extension activities to use after the reproducible:

- Success is in the bag with this fun working-backward activity. Cut out one green, six blue, and 12 red construction paper squares and place them in a paper lunch bag. Next, read aloud to your students the following problem: "There are twice as many red squares as blue squares. There are five more blue squares than green squares. There is one green square. How many red squares are in the bag?" Have your students solve the problem; then check their answers by having a student remove the squares from the bag and count the number of red squares *(12 red squares)*. Next, divide your students into pairs. Give each pair three different-colored sheets of construction paper, scissors, and a paper lunch bag. Instruct each pair to create a similar problem by cutting out colored squares, placing them in the bag, and writing a list of clues on an index card that will help another student determine how many of each color square is in the bag. Have pairs switch bags and clue cards and solve each other's problems. Afterward, collect the bags and place them at a center for individual exploration.

- Combine writing and math with this great idea! Write a math problem on the board from a recent assignment or test that uses the working-backward strategy. Instruct each student to write a step-by-step explanation of how he or she solved the problem. For an added twist, have students write their explanations in the form of a friendly letter to you! Students are sure to enjoy explaining their answers when they can do it in their own words.

Making "Cents" out of Working Backward

WOW! I love the mall!

Welcome to the Math Mall! Use the working-backward strategy to find answers to the following shopping situations. Write each answer in the blank provided.

The Bath Shop

3. At the end of her shift, Kristina had $540.12 in her cash register. During her shift she had only 3 customers. The first customer purchased $129.99 worth of items. The second customer spent twice as much as the first customer. The third customer paid $50.00 for her merchandise. How much money was in Kristina's register at the beginning of her shift?

Answer: _____

Sports R Us

1. Kathryn bought a soccer ball for $19.95 and a pair of sneakers that cost 3 times as much as the ball. She has $7.80 left in her backpack. How much money did she have before the purchases?

Answer: _____

FOOD COURT

2. Marvin did some taste testing in the food court. He bought a shake for $2.50 and a sub and soda combination for twice the amount of the shake. He also purchased a bag of fries for $2.99. Marvin has $3.10 left. How much money did Marvin have before he visited the food court?

Answer: _____

DJ Dan's Prize Booth

4. DJ Dan has brought his prize wheel to the mall today! Cindi won $102.04 with her spin. Curt won 3 times as much as Cindi. William's spin earned him half as much as Curt. If DJ Dan has $102.04 left to give away, how much prize money did he bring to the mall?

Answer: _____

Movie Theater
Ticket

5. After seeing a movie, Alvin has only $2.10 left of the birthday money his grandma sent. He bought a ticket for $4.25 and a drink for $1.75. He loved the movie so much that he bought a poster that cost $3.90. How much birthday money did Grandma send Alvin?

Answer: _____

THE CLOSET

6. Tasha bought a really cool blouse for 3 times as much as her scarf cost. Her scarf cost half as much as her hat. Her hat cost $10.00. How much did her blouse cost?

Answer: _____

Bonus Box: Kathryn wants to purchase 3 hair barrettes for $2.75 each. Does she have enough money left over from problem 1 to do so? Explain your answer in a brief paragraph on the back of this sheet that includes a number sentence to support your answer.

Lunchtime Logic

Increase your students' appetites for logical reasoning by bringing these problems to the table.

Purpose: To solve problems using logical reasoning

Students will do the following:

- interpret clues in word problems
- complete logic boxes by using the process of elimination
- design a logic box to match a corresponding problem

Materials for each student:

- copy of page 132
- pencil

Vocabulary to review:

- logical reasoning
- logic box
- process of elimination

Extension activities to use after the reproducible:

- Mystify your students with an activity that provides practice in using logical reasoning skills and number sense. Duplicate a class set of the hundreds chart on page 166. Then select one numeral on the chart as the mystery number. Create a set of clues that identify this numeral by eliminating the others. (*For example, if the mystery number is 27, the following clues can be used: The mystery number is an odd two-digit number. It is less than 45. It is a multiple of three. The sum of its digits is nine.*) Give each student a copy of the hundreds chart and a supply of dried beans or counters to use as markers. Read each clue aloud to your class. Have each student cover each numeral with a marker as it is eliminated. The first student to identify the mystery number is the winner. To extend the activity further, have each student write a set of clues for a mystery number of his choice.

- Write each equation shown in the art above on your chalkboard. Explain to your students that the shapes in the equations represent missing numerals. To complete each equation, they must use the following clues:
  Clue 1: Each numeral is between zero and nine.
  Clue 2: Each shape represents one numeral.
  Clue 3: Each numeral is a whole number.
  Write each clue underneath the equations you've written on the board. Then direct your students to use the clues and logical reasoning to complete each equation.
  ($\underline{2} + \underline{6} = 8$; $\underline{1} + \underline{3} = \underline{4}$; $\underline{8} - \underline{7} = 1$; $\underline{5} + 1 = 6$ or $\underline{1} + \underline{7} = \underline{8}$; $\underline{2} + \underline{6} = 8$; $\underline{4} - \underline{3} = 1$; $\underline{5} + \underline{1} = \underline{6}$)

Lunchtime Logic

Benny, Bobby, Barbara, Betty, and Biff met at the Backyard Barbecue Barn for a bite to eat. However, Wanda the waitress was having a really rotten day and accidentally mixed up all of their orders. For each problem below, use the clues and logic boxes to help you sort out their orders. Put a ✓ in each box that is true and an X in each box that is not true.

1. Use the following clues to sort out each friend's sandwich order.

    Clue 1: Biff doesn't eat beef or pork.
    Clue 2: Bobby did not order sausage.
    Clue 3: Barbara prefers her meat sliced.
    Clue 4: Betty did not order sausage or chopped beef.

	chopped beef	chicken	sliced beef	sausage	ribs
Benny					
Bobby					
Barbara					
Betty					
Biff					

2. As Wanda was walking to the table with the drink orders, she tripped and dropped the tray. Luckily, all the drinks landed right side up! Use the following clues to help Wanda distribute the drinks to the correct persons.

	Betty	Barbara	Benny	Bobby	Biff
soda					
fruit punch					
lemonade					
chocolate shake					
water					

Clue 1: None of the boys ordered fruit-flavored drinks.
Clue 2: Biff cannot drink carbonated drinks.
Clue 3: Bobby loves chocolate.
Clue 4: Betty prefers tart-tasting drinks with barbecue.

3. It's not surprising that Wanda mixed up the side dish orders too! Use the following clues to figure out who ordered which side dish.

    Clue 1: Benny can't eat fried foods or corn products.
    Clue 2: Bobby's favorite vegetable is corn.
    Clue 3: Barbara is trying to eat healthily.
    Clue 4: Biff likes to pour ketchup on top of his side dish.

	barbecued beans	hush puppies	tossed salad	corn	french fries
Benny					
Bobby					
Barbara					
Betty					
Biff					

Solve the problem below by constructing a logic box on the back of this page.

4. Due to all the mishaps, each friend received a free dessert. Wanda brought the following desserts to the table: strawberry pie, blackberry cobbler, chocolate delight, ice cream, and apple pie. Use the following clues to determine who ordered which dessert.

    Clue 1: Neither Bobby nor Biff likes pie.
    Clue 2: Biff's dessert melted all over his hands.
    Clue 3: Benny is allergic to berries.
    Clue 4: Betty only eats chocolate desserts.

Bonus Box: On another sheet of paper, use the same characters to develop a logic problem similar to the ones above. Then give your problem to a classmate to solve.

Won't You Be My Neighbor?

Let logical reasoning be your students' guide as they locate and label buildings and street names on a city block!

Purpose: To solve problems using map skills and logical reasoning

Students will do the following:

- use directional clues and a compass rose to correctly label houses and streets on a map
- use the process of elimination

Materials for each student:

- copy of page 134
- pencil

Vocabulary to review:

- cardinal directions
- intermediate directions
- compass rose
- across, opposite, beside, between
- corner, block

Main St.

Elm St.

What part of town do you live in?

Extension activities to use after the reproducible:

- Turn your students into budding cartographers with the following activity. Divide your students into pairs. Give each pair two sheets of drawing paper. Have each pair design a map on one sheet of paper that contains symbols for streets and buildings but no names. Then instruct the pair to list the names of the buildings and streets at the top of the other sheet of paper. Next, have the pair write a list of clues underneath the list of names for how to label the blank map. Instruct the pair to make an answer key for its map on the back of the clue page. Have each group trade its blank map and list of clues with another pair. Tell each pair to use the list of clues to label the blank map and then turn the clue sheet over to compare the labeled map with the answer key.

- Let students show how well they know the local terrain with the following activity. Divide your students into pairs. Give each pair a sheet of paper and a local map of your city, town, or community. Instruct each pair to pick a starting point (Point A) and an ending point (Point B) on the map. Instruct the pair to write the name of Point A on the front of the sheet of paper and write the name of Point B on the back of the sheet. Then, underneath the name of Point A, have each pair write a series of direction clues describing how to get from Point A to Point B. Next, have each pair trade its clue page with another pair. Instruct each pair to follow the clues carefully to get to Point B. Instruct the pair to check its answer by flipping the clue page over to see if the name of Point B matches where the pair ended up on the map.

Name_____

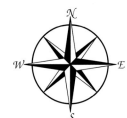

Won't You Be My Neighbor?

Use the clues, the compass rose, and logical reasoning to help you label the map for each problem below.

1. **Clue 1:** Streets running north and south are named for trees.
   Clue 2: Ray lives at the corner of Oak Rd. and Shoffner Blvd.
   Clue 3: Amy does not live on Birch St.
   Clue 4: Susan lives at the northeast corner of the block.
   Clue 5: Hefflin Ln. is north of Shoffner Blvd.
   Clue 6: Steve lives south of Susan.

2. **Clue 1:** Dawn lives at the northeast corner of South St. and Orange Ln.
   Clue 2: The streets that begin with vowels run north and south.
   Clue 3: Brian does not live on Eagle St.
   Clue 4: Jordan lives at the corner of South St. and Eagle St.
   Clue 5: Brittany lives at the corner of Eagle St. and Parklawn Rd.

3. **Clue 1:** Paul lives at the northeast corner of Parker St. and Sunnyway Blvd.
   Clue 2: Stacey lives on the opposite side of the street from Shawn.
   Clue 3: Sherri lives on Sunnyway Blvd. directly across from Paul.
   Clue 4: Nancy lives between Sherri and Shawn.
   Clue 5: Ed does not live beside Paul.
   Clue 6: Sunnyway Blvd. runs east and west.

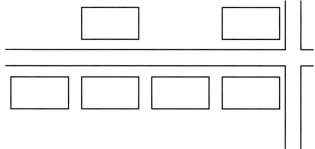

4. **Clue 1:** Oscar does not live on Broad St., but he does live east of Twiggy.
   Clue 2: Sylvester lives on the west corner of Broad St. and Morningside Ln.
   Clue 3: Felix is on the opposite side of the street from Sylvester.
   Clue 4: Twiggy lives north of Sylvester.

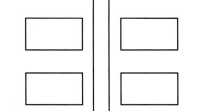

5. **Clue 1:** Darby, Danny, Drew, Dana, Danielle, and Darwin all live in separate houses on the same street.
   Clue 2: Darby lives west of Danny.
   Clue 3: Drew lives in the house that is furthest east.
   Clue 4: Danny lives west of Dana and east of Darby.
   Clue 5: Danielle lives on the east side of Dana.
   Clue 6: Darwin lives between Drew and Danielle.

Bonus Box: On the back of this page, create a new map for problem 1. Use the same character and street names, but change the location of each person's house. Then write a new set of clues for the new map. Trade your new map and clues with a partner to solve.

Logical Lineup

Your students will be eager beavers, wanting to try their hands at acting out these logical reasoning problems!

Purpose: To solve word problems by acting them out

Students will do the following:

- interpret clues in word problems
- act out situations using name cards

Materials for each student:

- copy of page 136
- pencil
- scissors
- glue

Vocabulary to review:

- in common
- attributes
- figures
- shapes
- classify

Extension activities to use after the reproducible:

- This activity might just help you discover some aspiring artists in your classroom! Provide students with six different-colored pattern blocks (or cubes). Instruct each student to arrange them on his desk or table. Then instruct him to write a series of clues on a sheet of paper that explains how to build or create his design. Next, have each student swap pattern blocks or (cubes) and clues with a partner and attempt to act out the solution to the partner's clues by trying to rebuild the design.

- A star is born! Turn each student into an actor with the following activity. Divide your students into groups of five. Instruct each group to act out each problem to find its solution.

Problem 1: There are four athletes competing in the 100-yard dash. Each runner says hello to each of the other runners. How many hellos are said in all? *(12 hellos)*

Problem 2: John, Jeanelle, Beverly, Jackie, and Rita are preparing for their first track meet of the season. Before the first race, each runner shakes hands with every other runner on the team once. How many handshakes take place? *(ten handshakes)*

Problem 3: James, Rayna, Jenny, Troy, and Duncan are sitting by the track waiting for the next race. Duncan is sitting to the left of James. James is sitting directly to the left of Troy. Rayna is sitting between Troy and Jenny. In what order are they sitting? *(Duncan, James, Troy, Rayna, Jenny)*

Logical Lineup

Directions: Cut out each name card at the bottom of the page. Solve each problem below by using the cards to act it out.

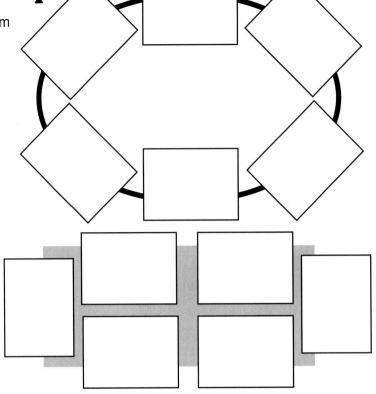

1. Some of Mrs. Burnett's students have formed a circle to play dodgeball. Use the name cards and the clues below to help you correctly label where each student is standing on the dodgeball circle.
Clues: Sue and Joe are across from each other. Christopher is in between 2 girls. Gail is standing beside Sue. Joe is standing beside another boy.

2. The 6 classmates are seated at a lunch table together. Use the name cards and the clues below to help you correctly label where each student is sitting.
Clues: Khristy and Christopher are sitting at each end of the table. Mike is sitting to Christopher's right. Sue is sitting to Khristy's left. Joe is sitting directly across from Mike. Gail is sitting beside Joe.

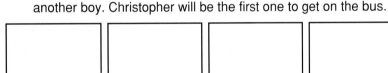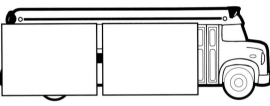

3. The 6 classmates are waiting patiently in a line for the school bus. Use the name cards and the clues below to help you correctly label where each student is standing,
Clues: Sue is the last one in line. Gail is behind the first student in line. Mike is in front of Khristy. Joe is in front of another boy. Christopher will be the first one to get on the bus.

4. Even though they're all fifth graders, the friends' ages differ. Use the name cards and the clues below to help you correctly order each student from youngest to oldest.
Clues: Mike is older than Sue, but younger than Khristy. Gail is the youngest. Joe is younger than Christopher, but older than Khristy. Christopher is the oldest.

Youngest   **Oldest**

5. All 6 students are in the science club at school. The club is having its picture taken for the yearbook. Use the clues below to help you determine where each student sits or stands for the photograph. Then, on the back of this sheet, glue the cutout name cards in 2 rows in the correct order. Label each row either "Standing" or "Sitting."
Clues: The students are in 2 rows. The front row is sitting; the back row is standing. Joe is in the back row. Christopher is not in the same row as Gail. Gail is in the middle of the front row. Khristy is between Joe and Christopher. Mike is to Gail's right. Sue is in front of Christopher.

Khristy   Gail   Sue   Joe   Christopher   Mike

School Supply Shopping Spree

Turn your students into smart shoppers by having them use the guess-and-check strategy to solve these real-life math problems!

Purpose: To solve problems using the guess-and-check strategy

Students will do the following:

- use guess and check to determine the cost of particular items
- add and subtract money
- use guess and check to determine the total amount of goods purchased

Materials for each student:

- copy of page 138
- pencil

Vocabulary to review:

- guess and check
- possible
- enough

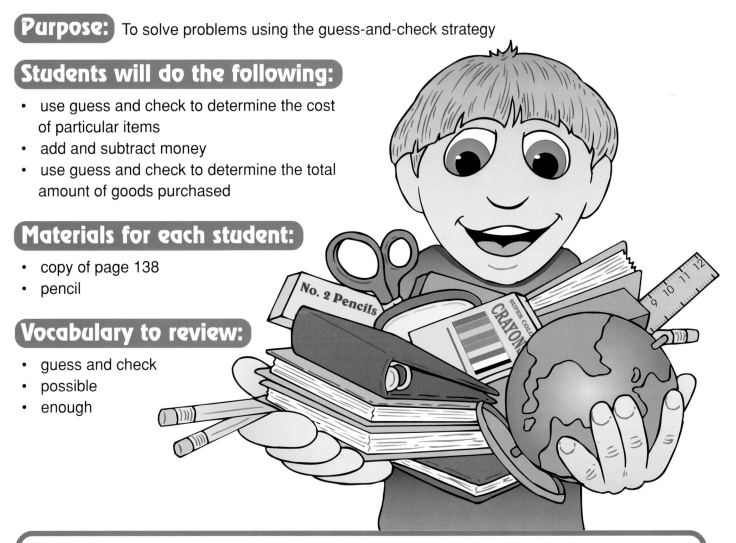

Extension activities to use after the reproducible:

- Make the guess-and-check problem-solving strategy come to life with this fun number game! Draw a large circle on the chalkboard and divide it into fourths. Number the sections 4, 5, 6, and 7. Then write the numeral 20 beside the circle. Next, have each student imagine that the circle is a spinner. Instruct each student to guess which numbers the spinner would need to land on using only four spins to equal 20. *(The student could spin a 4 twice and a 6 twice, or he could spin a 5 twice and a 4 and a 6 each once.)* Replace the numeral 20 with 22 and repeat the process. *(The student could spin a 4, 5, 6, and 7 each once, or he could spin a 6 twice and a 5 twice.)* To extend the activity, repeat the process with other numbers selected by your students.

- Keep students guessing with this fun activity! Have each student list four two-digit numbers on the back of a sheet of paper. Next, have him write down three or four clues to identify each number on the front of the same sheet of paper. Have each student switch his list of clues with a partner. Then instruct the students in each pair to solve each other's number clues and then flip the sheets over to see if their guesses are correct. After completing this activity, place the students' lists of numbers and clues at a math center to be completed independently.

School Supply Shopping Spree

Someone has stolen all the price tags from the school store. Help Mr. Pennypincher straighten out the mess before he opens for business!

Directions: Read each clue below and use the guess-and-check strategy to identify the cost of each item. Write each answer in the blank provided.

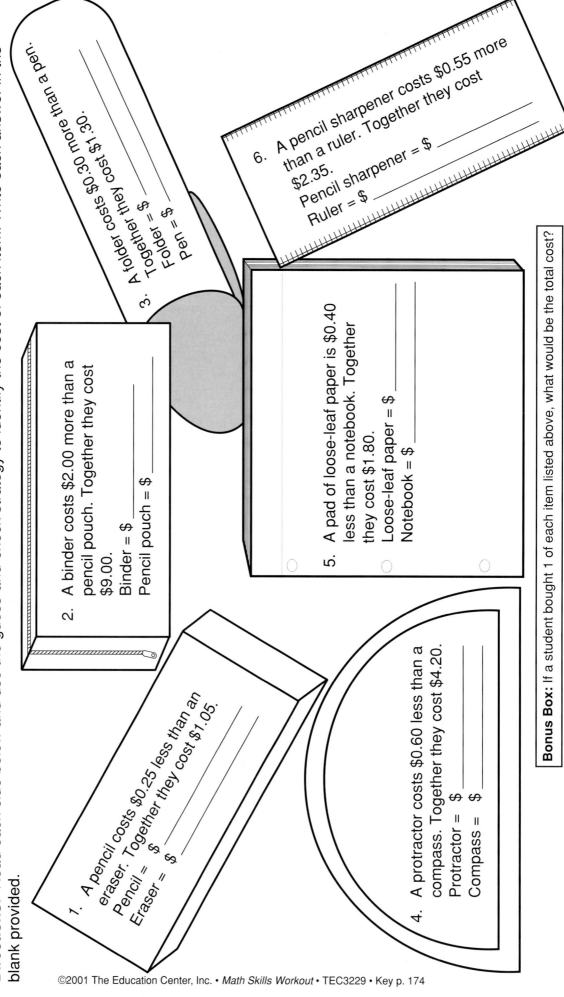

3. A folder costs $0.30 more than a pen.
   Together they cost $1.30.
   Together they cost = $ _____
   Folder = $ _____
   Pen = $ _____

6. A pencil sharpener costs $0.55 more than a ruler. Together they cost $2.35.
   Pencil sharpener = $ _____
   Ruler = $ _____

2. A binder costs $2.00 more than a pencil pouch. Together they cost $9.00.
   Binder = $ _____
   Pencil pouch = $ _____

5. A pad of loose-leaf paper is $0.40 less than a notebook. Together they cost $1.80.
   Loose-leaf paper = $ _____
   Notebook = $ _____

1. A pencil costs $0.25 less than an eraser. Together they cost $1.05.
   Pencil = $ _____
   Eraser = $ _____

4. A protractor costs $0.60 less than a compass. Together they cost $4.20.
   Protractor = $ _____
   Compass = $ _____

Bonus Box: If a student bought 1 of each item listed above, what would be the total cost?

©2001 The Education Center, Inc. • *Math Skills Workout* • TEC3229 • Key p. 174

Royal Riddles!

Purpose: To solve problems using the guess-and-check strategy

Students will do the following:

- solve number riddles
- use clues to eliminate possible answers
- apply number-sense skills

Materials for each student:

- copy of page 140
- pencil
- scratch paper

Vocabulary to review:

- sum
- multiple
- ones
- tens
- prime
- palindrome
- divisible

I'm thinking of a number that's a palindrome and is less than 250 but more than 240.

Hmm . . . Could it be 242?

Extension activities to use after the reproducible:

- Turn your math book into a thrilling mystery with this fun activity! Write the following problem on the board: "Ben opened his math book once to two pages. The sum of the page numbers is 245. What are the two pages?" *(122 and 123)* Have students randomly open their math books and write problems just like this one. Then have each student exchange problems with a partner and solve his partner's problem.

- Make lunch a scavenger hunt with this great idea! Duplicate your cafeteria menu and distribute a copy to each student. Have each student assign every menu item a price (if prices aren't already included). Then have each student make up five different combinations of two to four food items. After finding the total cost of each combination, have him write it on the back of his menu and on a separate sheet of paper. Finally, have each student exchange menus with a partner and try to list the combinations of food items that match his partner's totals.

Royal Riddles!

The Queen of Computation has given you a challenge: "Answer my riddles and become a royal problem solver! The more riddles you solve, the more points you earn. Earn at least 250 points and the job of royal problem solver is yours!"

Directions: Read each set of clues; then use the guess-and-check strategy to solve the riddle. Write your answer on the line provided; then have your teacher tally your score.

10 points
- 2-digit number
- sum of digits is 9
- multiple of 5
- tens digit is smaller than ones digit

1. _____

20 points
- less than 100
- divisible by 5
- multiple of 11

2. _____

30 points
- less than 78
- more than 50
- multiple of 4
- sum of digits is 10

3. _____

40 points
- 3-digit number
- less than 150
- more than 100
- sum of digits is 10
- prime number

4. _____

50 points
- 3-digit number
- less than 300
- greater than 200
- palindrome
- sum of digits is 8

5. _____

60 points
- less than 860
- more than 840
- even number
- sum of digits is 18

6. _____

70 points
- 4-digit palindrome
- less than 1,500
- more than 1,200
- odd number
- divisible by 3

7. _____

80 points
- less than 1,580
- more than 1,450
- multiple of 25, but not 10
- sum of digits is even

8. _____

90 points
- less than 1,010
- more than 960
- divisible by 6
- sum of digits is less than 5

9. _____

My Royal Problem Solver score is _____

Bonus Box: Create a number riddle like the ones above based on your Royal Problem Solver score. Then have a friend solve it.

Tuning In to Tables

Help students add the make-a-table strategy to their list of greatest problem-solving hits!

Purpose: To solve problems by making a table

Students will do the following:

- identify number patterns
- complete two different types of tables
- construct appropriate tables
- use data in tables to solve problems

Materials for each student:

- copy of page 142
- loose-leaf paper
- pencil

Vocabulary to review:

- ordinals: third, sixth, etc.
- for every
- schedule

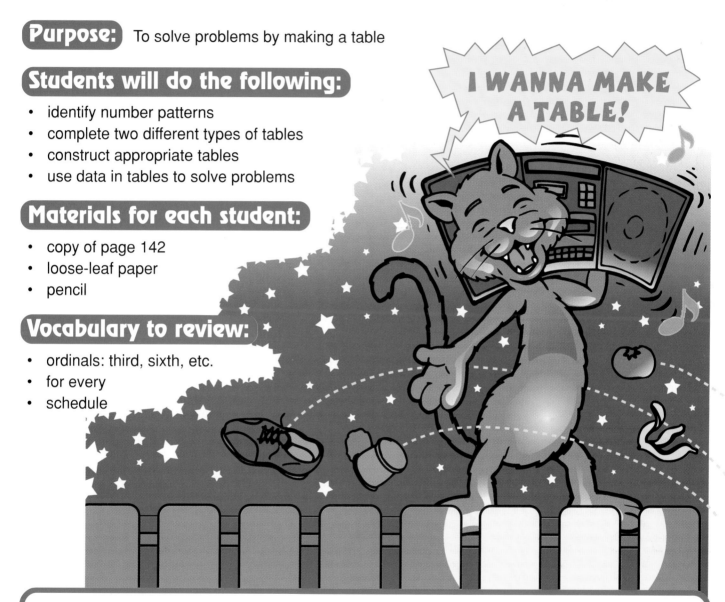

I WANNA MAKE A TABLE!

Extension activities to use after the reproducible:

- Turn the tables on students by having them use the make-a-table strategy to make an interesting comparison about two daily activities. Direct each student to write down the number of hours he spent watching television yesterday and then the number of hours he read (for example, "watched television four hours and read two hours"). Then have him make a table to determine the number of hours he will have read after watching 20 hours of television.

- Opportunities for making tables are everywhere! Have each student count either the number of windows, computers, or bulletin boards in your classroom. Then challenge her to use that information to create a problem using the make-a-table strategy. For example: Each classroom has three computers for every 20 students. If our school has 200 students, how many computers do we have? *(30)* Then have each student trade her problem with a partner and solve.

Tuning In to Tables

The most requested song at radio station WMAK recently has been "I Wanna Make a Table." Help send this song to the top of the listeners' chart by solving the problems below. Each one can be solved by making a table. Be sure to write each solution in a complete sentence.

I WANNA MAKE A TABLE!

1. The Rockets's new hit, "You Send Me to the Stars," has been requested a lot this week. On the first day of the week, callers requested this song 5 times. They requested it 12 times on the second day, 10 times on the third day, and 17 times on the fourth day. If this pattern continues, how many times will this song be requested on the tenth day?

Day	1	2	3	4	5	6	7	8	9	10
Requests										

Solution: _____

2. Best friends Dan and Derek are DJs who work at radio station WMAK. This month's schedule has Dan working on the first Sunday and every other day after that. Derek is scheduled to work on Tuesdays, Fridays, and Saturdays. How many days during the next 2 weeks will the friends work on the same day? If this pattern continues, how many days will the friends work together by the end of the fourth week?

Day														
Dan														
Derek														

Solution: _____

Solve each problem below by constructing a table on the back of this page. Then write each solution on the line provided.

3. WMAK just wrapped up a 10-day contest in which CDs were given away. On the first day of the contest, 20 CDs were given away. Thirty-two CDs were given away on the second day, 44 on the third day, and 56 on the fourth day. If this pattern continued, how many CDs were given away during the entire 10-day period?

Solution: _____

4. According to a WMAK listener poll, there are 5 alternative music fans for every 8 hip-hop fans. Based on this poll, how many hip-hop fans would there be if there were 25 alternative music fans?

Solution: _____

5. WMAK's latest contest offers $15.00 cash to the listener who can give the correct titles of 3 songs played on fast speed. If no one wins on the first day, another $15.00 will be added to the total each day until someone wins! It is now day 8, and there is still no winner. What is the value of the cash prize now?

Solution: _____

 ©2001 The Education Center, Inc. • *Math Skills Workout* • TEC3229 • Key p. 174

Taking Problem Solving for a Ride!

Send students on the ride of their lives as they make and use tables to solve problems!

Purpose: To solve problems by making a table

Students will do the following:

- find patterns in whole numbers
- compare groups of data
- complete and construct tables

Materials for each student:

- copy of page 144
- pencil

Vocabulary to review:

- pattern
- ordinal numbers: first, second, fifth, tenth, etc.
- compare
- construct

Extension activities to use after the reproducible:

- Let toothpicks help your students pick their way to success with the make-a-table strategy. First, show students how to construct a 2 x 4 rectangle from toothpicks. Next, give each student a pile of toothpicks and have him duplicate your rectangle. Then direct him to construct another rectangle that is 3 x 6 and to identify the pattern that is developing *(width increases by one and length increases by two)*. Then have each student use his toothpicks to make a table to find the width of a rectangle whose length is ten toothpicks *(five toothpicks)*.

- Review the make-a-table strategy by having students stir up a delicious and nutritious treat! Write the following recipe for "Make-a-Table Trail Mix" on the board: For eight servings, mix one cup each of shelled peanuts, raisins, M&M's® candies, and Honey Nut Cheerios® cereal. Challenge each student to make and complete a table showing how much of each ingredient they would need to make enough of this snack for the entire class. After checking students' tables, set out the ingredients along with a few supplies for mixing and sharing (provided by parents ahead of time). Then have students mix the ingredients and snack away!

Taking Problem Solving for a Ride!

Porcupine Pete and his friends work at a local theme park. Their boss is rather particular about park-related data and insists that it be kept in tables. So the make-a-table strategy comes in handy for Pete and company. Help make their jobs a little easier by solving the problems below. Each one can be solved by making a table. Be sure to write each solution in a complete sentence.

1. Of the first 18 people entering the park last Saturday, Porcupine Pete noticed that every third person rode the roller coaster and every sixth person rode the wild water ride. How many of these 18 park visitors rode both the roller coaster and the water ride?   ROLLER COASTER   WILD WATER RIDE

Visitors	1	2	3	4	5	6	7	8	9	10	11	12	13	14	15	16	17	18
Roller Coaster																		
Water Ride																		

Solution: _____

2. Penny and Patty sold hamburgers, hot dogs, and fries at the concession stand last Saturday. The girls noticed that 3 hot dogs and 2 fries were bought for every 7 hamburgers they sold. At this rate, how many hot dogs and fries had the girls sold when their hamburger sales reached 63?

Hamburgers	7								
Hot Dogs	3								
Fries	2								

Solution: _____

**Solve each problem below by constructing a table on the back of this page.
Then write each solution on the line provided.**

3. On Friday, Penelope Porcupine was in charge of 30 park visitors who played the same 3 games: the softball pitch, the dart throw, and the ring toss. She noticed that every 5th person won at softball, every 10th person the dart throw, and every 15th person the ring toss. How many of the 30 players won all 3 games?

Solution: _____

4. Dolly, the theme park's star dolphin, is on a roll with her performances! The first week, she jumped through 12 hoops during the water show. She jumped through 19 hoops during the second week, 26 hoops the third week, 33 hoops the fourth week, and 40 hoops the fifth week. At this rate, through how many hoops will Dolly jump during the tenth week?

Solution: _____

5. Of the 24 park visitors waiting to ride the Tilt-a-Whirl, Porcupine Paul noticed that every fourth visitor wore sunglasses and every eighth visitor wore a hat. How many of these 24 visitors wore both sunglasses and a hat?

Solution: _____

This Way to Outer Space

Enhance your students' drawing and problem-solving skills with these out-of-this-world problems!

Purpose: To solve problems by drawing pictures

Students will do the following:

- draw a map following directional clues
- draw a picture to illustrate a solution
- use maps to calculate distances and direction

Materials for each student:

- copy of page 146
- pencil

Vocabulary to review:

- direction
- north, south, east, west
- Venn diagram

Extension activities to use after the reproducible:

- See how familiar your students are with roads in your community with the following activity. Select a location (a business, theater, mall, library, etc.) near your school. Divide your students into pairs. Instruct each pair to draw a map showing the shortest route from school to the designated location. Have each pair show its map to the rest of the class and explain why it feels this is the shortest route. If possible, plot out the various routes on a local map and have students use the map's mileage scale to figure out which route actually is the shortest.

- Show students how drawing a Venn diagram can help them solve problems. Write the following problems on the board and have your students solve them by drawing a Venn diagram for both.

  Twenty-two space creatures are zooming around in new spaceships. Fourteen of the creatures are wearing helmets, six are wearing goggles, and four are wearing both helmets and goggles. How many space creatures are wearing neither helmets nor goggles? *(Six creatures are wearing neither helmets nor goggles.)*

  Fifteen kids are on Mr. Spadafino's swim team. Eight are wearing swim caps, five have blue towels, and three wearing swim caps have blue towels. How many kids on Mr. Spadafino's swim team have neither a swim cap nor a blue towel? *(Five kids on the team have neither a swim cap nor a blue towel.)*

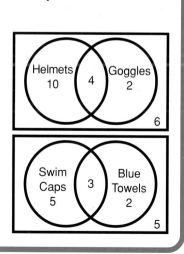

This Way to Outer Space

Gallatica is an extremely busy galaxy. Carefully read each problem below. On another sheet of paper draw a picture to help you solve each problem. Then write each answer in the blank provided.

1. Starry lives on the planet Nebula. She left home and flew 6 miles east to visit a friend. She then flew 8 miles south and stopped at the spaceship wash. Next, Starry flew 3 miles west, 3 miles north, and then 3 miles west to reach her school. If Starry goes straight home from school, how many miles and in what direction will she need to fly?

    Answer: _____

2. Quasar wanted to play laser tag with some of his friends. He hopped in his spacemobile and flew 2 planets west to pick up his friend, Pulsar. Then he flew 5 planets east to pick up his friend, Comet. Comet lives on the last planet in the solar system. Finally, Quasar flew 7 planets west to pick up Rocky. Rocky lives on the first planet in the galaxy. What is the total number of planets in Quasar's solar system?

    Answer: _____

3. On the passenger starship *The Destiny,* the captain lost her log on the main deck. She walked down the deck 5 doors looking for the log, but no luck. Then she turned around and walked up the deck 6 doors to the end, but still no log. Next, she turned around and walked down the deck 4 doors, with no luck. Finally, she walked down the deck 8 more doors to the other end and found her log! What is the total number of doors on the deck?

    Answer: _____

4. The Great Space Race begins and ends in the same spot. The fliers travel 50 kilometers west to the first fuel stop. Next, they fly 30 kilometers north to the second fuel stop. Then they fly 20 kilometers east and 10 kilometers south to the third fuel stop. To get to the fourth fuel stop, the fliers must fly 30 kilometers east. How many more kilometers and in what direction does each flier need to travel in order to reach the finish line?

    Answer: _____

5. Rosie the Robot did some shopping at Saturn Shopping Center. She traveled down 5 stores to the bath shop. Then she turned around and traveled up 7 stores to the shoe store, which is at the end of the shopping center. Next, she turned around and traveled down 6 stores to the bookstore. Then she continued down the shopping center 6 more stores to the soda shop, which is at the other end of the shopping center. How many stores are at Saturn Shopping Center?

    Answer: _____

6. Cosmo left work to run a few errands. He flew 8 miles north to the spaceship rental office. Then he flew 12 miles east to Comet Cleaners. From there, he traveled 4 miles south and 8 miles west to get some lunch at McLaser's. Finally, he flew 4 miles south to the video disc store. If he flies straight back to work, how many miles and in what direction must he fly?

    Answer: _____

Bonus Box: On the back of this sheet, calculate the total distance traveled in number 1. Then do the same for number 4.

It's Party Time!

Help your students get the party started by finding solutions to these problems.

Purpose: To solve problems by drawing pictures

Students will do the following:

- draw pictures using descriptions given in word problems
- use drawings to solve problems
- write to explain thinking

Materials for each student:

- copy of page 148
- pencil

Vocabulary to review:

- vertical
- horizontal
- represent

Extension activities to use after reproducible:

- Break out the art supplies, and challenge the creative and the critical-thinking sides of each student's mind with the following draw-a-picture activity. Draw a design of five connecting squares on a sheet of paper; then duplicate a class supply of the design. Next, divide your students into pairs. Give each pair two copies of the design you've created, one paintbrush, and a set of watercolor paints. Instruct each pair to paint each square on one copy of the design a different color. Tell the pairs that they've just painted the solution to a problem. Next, instruct the pair to write a series of clues for its painted design. Have each pair trade clues with another pair. Instruct the students in each pair to follow the clues to help them paint the blank copy of the design. *(Instruct each pair to hold onto its painted design until the other pair has followed the clues and is ready to check its solution.)*

- Further extend students' use of the draw-a-picture strategy with the following activity. Divide your students into pairs and instruct them to draw pictures to solve the two problems below. Then instruct the pair to create two more draw-a-picture problems for another pair to solve.

  Problem 1: Out of 20 classrooms on Tammy's hallway at school, 12 classrooms on the east end have new carpet and 15 classrooms on the west end have new paint. How many classrooms have new carpet and new paint? *(seven classrooms)*

  Problem 2: There are 24 classroom doors along one hallway in Tom's school. Every other door (starting with the second door) has a poster on it. Every fourth door has a teacher's name on it, and every sixth door has a number on it. How many doors contain a poster, a teacher's name, and a number? *(two doors)*

It's Party Time!

Kathy is planning her birthday party. Although most plans are running smoothly, there are a few problems. Solve each problem below by drawing a picture in the box provided.

1. Kathy has ordered a beautiful cake. On top of the round cake in a circle are 6 flowers made of frosting. After each flower in the circle are 2 candles. If the number of candles represents Kathy's age, which birthday is Kathy celebrating?

Answer: _____

2. Kathy's mom is setting up tables for the party. Each table is large enough to seat 2 people on each side and 2 people on each end. The tables are arranged so that at least 1 end is touching the end of another table. There are 24 people coming to the party. How many tables will be needed?

Answer: _____

3. Kathy's mom has made a batch of crispy rice-cereal bars. Her treats are in a rectangular pan that measures 12" x 8". She will cut a vertical and horizontal line every 2 inches along the length and width of the pan. How many bars will each guest receive?

Answer: _____

4. Kathy's brother is cutting ribbon for presents. He has a piece of ribbon that is 10 feet long. How many cuts must he make to have pieces that measure 2 feet each?

Answer: _____

5. Kathy has made 24 special oatmeal cookies, 1 for each guest. The cookies are cooling in a horizontal row on a cooling rack. The first 14 cookies have chocolate chips, and the last 14 cookies have raisins. Every fourth cookie has nuts. How many cookies have both chocolate chips and raisins? How many cookies have chocolate chips, raisins, and nuts?

Answer: _____

Bonus Box: Kathy's mom just found out that 4 more guests are coming to the party. How can she cut the pan of crispy rice-cereal bars so that there will be enough to give each guest 1 bar? Draw a picture on the back of this page to show your answer.

Bushels of Pattern-Finding Fun

Not even one bad apple can be found in this challenging bunch of problems!

Purpose: To solve problems by identifying patterns

Students will do the following:

- identify number patterns in a word problem
- continue a pattern to find a solution

Materials for each student:

- copy of page 150
- pencil

Vocabulary to review:

- pattern
- possible
- enough

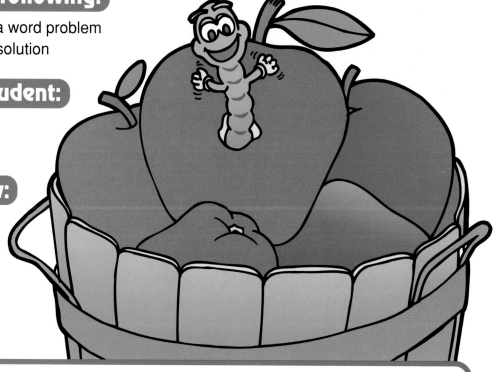

Extension activities to use after the reproducible:

- Identifying the *core* of a pattern helps students become aware of its structure. In some patterns the core repeats (2, 3, 4, 2, 3, 4,…), while in other patterns the core grows (2, 4, 6, 8, 10,…). Have your students identify the core of each pattern below. Then challenge each student to create a pattern for a classmate to solve by identifying the core.

12, 17, 14, 19, 16	(Core = add five, subtract three)
100, 125, 150, 175	(Core = add 25)
5, 12, 18, 23, 27, 30	(Core = add seven, add six, add five, etc.)
2, 6, 8, 24, 26, 78, 80	(Core = multiply by three, add two)

- Challenge your students to solve the following problem by identifying the core of the pattern and continuing the pattern.

  You've just been offered a new job, but you're not sure if you should accept the offer. On your first day you will be paid $1. Each day after that, your pay will be twice as much as the amount you received the previous day. What will your pay be on the 12th day?

Day	1	2	3	4	5	6	7	8	9	10	11	12
Amount Paid	$1	$2	$4	$8	$16	$32	$64	$128	$256	$512	$1,024	$2,048

Bushels of Pattern-Finding Fun

Wilbur Worm is working his way through the problems below.
Help Wilbur solve each problem by identifying the pattern.
Write the answer and pattern for each
problem in the blank provided.

1. Simon put 12 apples in 2 baskets, 18 apples in 3 baskets, and 24 apples in 4 baskets. Continuing this pattern, how many apples will he put in 6 baskets?

   Answer: _____

   Pattern: _____

   _____

2. Brittany can make 2 large apple pies using 15 apples, 4 pies using 30 apples, and 6 pies using 45 apples. How many apples will she need to make 10 pies?

   Answer: _____

   Pattern: _____

   _____

3. Mrs. Farmer sold 3 jars of apple jelly and 5 jars of apple butter on Monday, 6 jars of apple jelly and 10 jars of apple butter on Tuesday, and 9 jars of apple jelly and 15 jars of apple butter on Wednesday. If this trend continues, how many jars of apple jelly and apple butter will Mrs. Farmer sell on Thursday?

   Answer: _____

   Pattern: _____

   _____

4. Granny Smith picked 65 apples on Sunday, 50 apples on Monday, 55 apples on Tuesday, and 40 apples on Wednesday. At this rate, how many apples will she pick on Thursday?

   Answer: _____

   Pattern: _____

   _____

5. Mr. Delicious made 12 apple muffins and 6 quarts of applesauce on Saturday, 18 muffins and 12 quarts of applesauce on Sunday, and 24 muffins and 18 quarts of applesauce on Monday. If this pattern continues, how many muffins and quarts of applesauce will he make on Tuesday?

   Answer: _____

   Pattern: _____

   _____

Bonus Box: If Granny Smith continues to pick apples at the same rate through Saturday, what will be the total number of apples she picks for the week?

 ©2001 The Education Center, Inc. • *Math Skills Workout* • TEC3229 • Key p. 175

Sally's Sub Shop

Have your students construct tree diagrams to solve these tasty problems.

Purpose: To solve problems by constructing tree diagrams

Students will do the following:

- construct tree diagrams using data from word problems
- interpret data presented in tree diagrams

Materials for each student:

- copy of page 152
- pencil

Vocabulary to review:

- tree diagram
- combinations
- include

Extension activities to use after the reproducible:

- Give your students more practice constructing tree diagrams with these challenging problems.

    Problem 1: John has a blue shirt, a green shirt, a pair of tan pants, a pair of white pants, a pair of brown pants, a red jacket, and a yellow jacket. How many three-piece outfits can he make? *(John can make 12 different outfits.)*

    Problem 2: How many different three-letter code words can Lucy make using the letters X, Y, and Z if the code permits repetition of letters? *(Lucy can make 27 possible code words.)*

- Your students will enjoy creating this challenging math center. Divide your students into pairs. Give each pair one 8$\frac{1}{2}$" x 11" sheet of paper. Then tell each pair to fold its paper in half like a greeting card that lifts up. Next, instruct the pair to create an original problem that can be solved by constructing a tree diagram. Have the pair write the problem on the outside of the card and draw the completed tree diagram on the inside. Collect the cards and post them on a board so that the top half of the card can be lifted. Encourage students to visit the board during free time to solve the problems.

Sally's Sub Shop

Sally's Sub Shop provides so many selections that it's hard to keep things straight! Solve each problem below by creating a tree diagram.

1. Sally offers several cold sub lunch specials. You can choose from turkey, ham, or roast beef on white or wheat bread. Your sandwich comes with either mayo or mustard. Complete the tree diagram to find all the possible sandwich combinations; then answer each question below.

   MEAT   BREAD   CONDIMENT   SANDWICH

   How many sandwich combinations can you make? _____

   How many combinations include wheat bread and mustard? _____

   How many combinations include ham? _____

   _____

2. Sally's dinner specials include your choice of soup and sandwich. The soups are noodle, tomato, and vegetable. The sandwich choices are turkey and ham. Construct a tree diagram to show all the possible combinations.

   How many soup and sandwich combinations can be made? _____

   How many combinations include tomato soup? _____

3. Many people just stop in for dessert and a warm drink. Today Sally is serving carrot cake, sugar cookies, cheesecake, and hot cocoa or hot cider. Construct a tree diagram to display all the possible combinations.

   How many different dessert and hot drink combinations can be made? _____

   How many combinations include hot cocoa? _____

4. A popular item on the menu is Sally's Side Salad. In your side salad you can have tomatoes, cucumbers, or carrots. You can choose American cheese, Swiss cheese, or cheddar cheese. You can also choose between Italian dressing and ranch dressing. Construct a tree diagram to show all the possible combinations.

   How many different ways can you order Sally's Side Salad? _____

5. Sally also serves several hot sub meals. You can order a meatball sub, a ham and cheese sub, or a tuna melt. You can order your hot sandwich on Italian bread or a wheat roll. It also comes with potato, corn, or nacho chips. Show all the possible combinations on a tree diagram.

   How many different hot sub meals can you order at Sally's? _____

   How many hot sub meals include nacho chips? _____

   Bonus Box: Sally just added brownies to her dessert tray. Now how many possible combinations of dessert and hot drink can you order?

On the Fast Track

Have your students cross the finish line as winners with this activity on constructing Venn diagrams!

Purpose: To solve problems by constructing and interpreting Venn diagrams

Students will do the following:

- construct Venn diagrams with three intersecting circles
- correctly place data on a Venn diagram
- interpret data displayed in a Venn diagram

Materials for each student:

- copy of page 154
- pencil

Vocabulary to review:

- Venn diagram
- intersecting

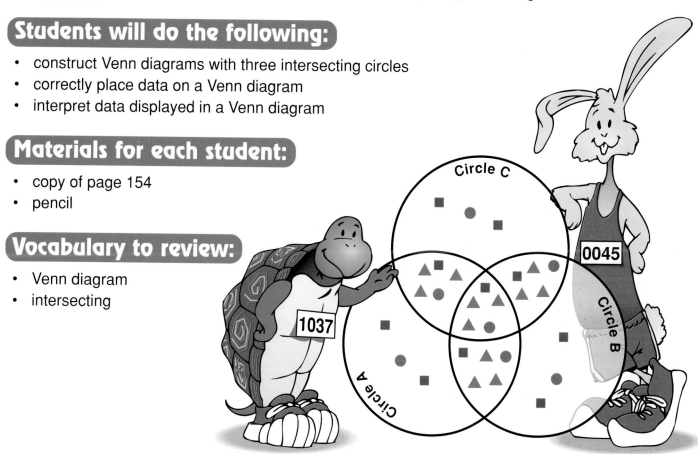

Extension activities to use after the reproducible:

- Both you and your students will love using this reusable Venn diagram. Take a large gray or white plastic trash bag and cut it along both side seams. Lay the bag on the floor and trace three intersecting circles on the bag using a permanent marker and a large bucket or a wastebasket. Hang the Venn diagram up in your classroom. Label three sentence strips, each with a different category related to your students, such as blue jeans, white shirt and sneakers. Then tape each strip by a different circle on the diagram. Next, give each student a sticky note and instruct him to place it in the appropriate section of the diagram. Together, interpret the data collected on the Venn diagram. Leave the Venn diagram up and repeat the activity regularly with different categories.

- Challenge your students with the following fun Venn diagram problem. Draw the Venn diagram above on the board using colored chalk or on chart paper using markers. Then have each student answer the following questions.
  How many squares are in all three circles? *(one square)*
  How many circles are in Circle B? *(four circles)*
  How many triangles are in both Circle A and Circle C only? *(three triangles)*
  How many squares are in both Circle A and Circle B only? *(one square)*
  Now have each student write a list of his own questions about the diagram to swap with a friend to answer.

On the Fast Track

The Glenn Dale Gators held a fifth-grade track meet. Help organize the students who competed in the events by using and constructing Venn diagrams with 3 intersecting circles.

1. Use the Venn diagram below to help you answer the following questions.

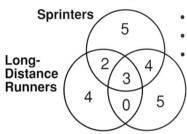

- How many fifth graders are sprinters? _____
- How many fifth graders competed in all 3 events? _____
- How many fifth graders competed in just 1 event? _____

2. Complete the diagram at the right by using the information below. Then use the diagram to help you answer each question.

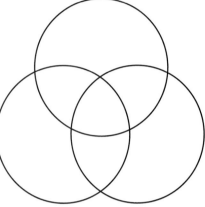

Three students competed in just the shotput and the discus. Five students competed in just the javelin. Six students signed up to compete in just the shotput. Four students competed in just the shotput and the javelin, but not the discus. Fourteen students total competed in the shotput. Seventeen students total competed in the javelin. Twelve students total competed in the discus.

- How many students competed in all 3 events? _____
- How many students competed in both the javelin and discus, but not the shotput? _____
- How many students competed in just the discus? _____

3. On the back of this sheet, construct a Venn diagram with 3 intersecting circles using the data below. Then use the diagram to help you answer each question.

The track meet was a great success! Fifteen medals were given on each level: gold, silver, and bronze. Seven students won just a bronze. No one won just a bronze and silver. Four students won just a gold and a silver. Three students won just a gold and bronze.

- How many people won all 3 medals? _____
- How many people won just a gold medal? _____
- How many people won just a silver medal? _____

4. On the back of this sheet, construct a Venn diagram with 3 intersecting circles using the data below. Then use the diagram to help you answer each question.

A group of 10 students competed in each of these events: 50-,100-, and 200-yard dash. Four students ran just the 100-yard dash. Four students ran just the 200-yard dash. One student ran in all 3. One student ran in both the 50-and 100-yard dashes, but not the 200-yard dash.

- How many students ran in both the 100- and 200-yard dash, but not the 50-yard dash?

  _____
- How many students ran in both the 50- and 200-yard dash, but not the 100-yard dash?

  _____
- How many students ran in just the 50-yard dash? _____

Bonus Box: How would the answers change in problem 1 if 7 students had competed in all 3 events instead of only 3?

A Monster of a List

Purpose: To solve problems by making lists

Students will do the following:

- arrange items in a given order
- list all possible combinations of a group of items
- use reasoning skills

Materials for each student:

- copy of page 156
- pencil

Vocabulary to review:

- combination
- order
- possible

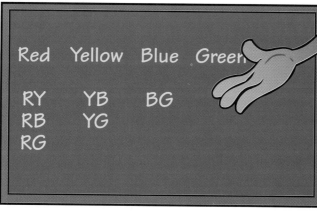

Extension activities to use after the reproducible:

- Learning how to make a list will be in the bag with this activity! Place four different-colored crayons in a paper bag. Then list the colors on the board. Direct each student to use the make-a-list strategy to solve the two problems below:

  Problem 1: Each crayon is picked out of the bag, one at a time. In how many possible orders could the crayons be picked from the bag? *(24 different combinations)*
  Problem 2: Two crayons are picked from the bag and then replaced. How many possible combinations of crayon pairs could be picked from the bag? *(six different pairs)*

- Challenge each student to list all the possible combinations of school meals that can be made from three different kinds of sandwiches (a sloppy joe, a hamburger, and a grilled cheese sandwich), two different kinds of fruit (an apple and an orange), and two different kinds of milk (chocolate and skim). *(12 different combinations)*

A Monster of a List

Max, Molly, Marvin, Missy, and Minny Monster are making their way to the Goosebump Grill for a midnight meal. As usual, there are many menu combinations from which to choose. Make an organized list to solve each problem below.

1. Molly Monster can't decide which kind of sandwich to order. She can choose either ham, roast beef, or turkey. Her bread choices are wheat and rye. List all the possible meat and bread combinations Molly can order.

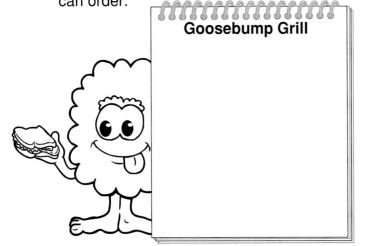

Goosebump Grill

2. Marvin Monster's mouth is watering for some pasta. He can choose from ravioli, macaroni, and spaghetti. The sauce choices are tomato, cream, and pesto. List all the possible pasta and sauce combinations Marvin can order.

Goosebump Grill

Write the lists for problems 4 and 5 on the back of this sheet.

3. Minny Monster plans to skip her midnight meal and go straight to dessert. There are 5 different desserts on the menu: chocolate sundae, butterscotch pudding, toffee, banana cream pie, and strawberry sorbet. If Minny decides to eat 2 desserts, list all the possible dessert combinations she can order.

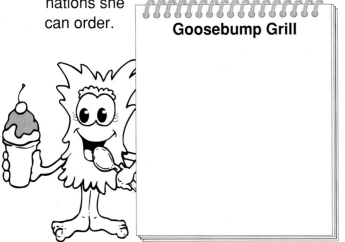

Goosebump Grill

4. Missy Monster plans to choose from the same pasta and sauce possibilities as Marvin. She also wants to add a cheese topping. She can add mozzarella or Romano. List all the possible pasta, sauce, and cheese combinations she can order.

5. Max Monster does not eat meat. The meatless dishes to choose from are a veggie pita, a peanut butter croissant, and a cheese enchilada. He also wants to order a side dish and drink. His side dish choices are a salad, rice, and soup. For a drink he can order tea, cola, or milk. List all the possible meatless dish, side dish, and drink combinations Max can order.

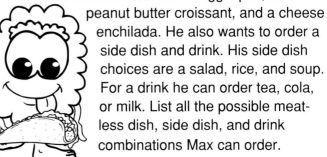

Bonus Box: In problem 5 above, how many menu combinations include a peanut butter croissant? How many include tea? How many include both a salad and tea? List your answers on the back of this page.

A New Spin on Making a List

Show your students a new spin on making an organized list!

Purpose: To solve problems by making organized lists

Students will do the following:

- use a spinner to randomly select prices under $1
- make organized lists of possible coin combinations to equal specific amounts

Materials for each student:

- copy of page 158
- pencil
- paper clip

Vocabulary to review:

- quarter, nickel, dime
- organized list
- possible combinations

Let's spin the wheel!

The Snack Wheel

Extension activities to use after the reproducible:

- Have each student gather four items, such as a ruler, pen, tack, and crayon. Divide the students into pairs. Instruct one member of the pair to challenge the other member to list all the possible ways the four items can be arranged in left-to-right order. (See the example below.) Then repeat the process with the other student's four items.

RPTC	RPCT	RTCP	RTPC	RCPT	RCTP
PTCR	PTRC	PRTC	PCTR	PCRT	PRCT
TCRP	TCPR	TRPC	TRCP	TPCR	TPRC
CRPT	CRTP	CPTR	CPRT	CTRP	CTPR

- Turn your students into fashion plates with the following activity. Display two different types of shirts, two different pairs of pants, and two different pairs of shoes. Then challenge each student to list all the possible combinations of outfits that can be made from two different shirts, two pairs of pants, and two different pairs of shoes. *(eight different outfits)*

A New Spin on Making a List

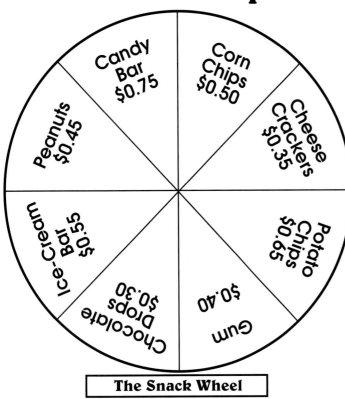

The Snack Wheel

Freddie and each of his 4 friends get a chance to spin the snack wheel each day. The snack the spinner lands on is the snack the person spinning gets to purchase that day. Make a spinner out of a pencil and paper clip as shown. Next, spin the wheel for each person below. Write the name of the snack and its price in the blanks provided. Then, on another sheet of paper, make an organized list of all the different coin combinations the person can use to pay for the snack using quarters, dimes, and/ or nickels. Write the total number of combinations for each price in the blank provided.

1. Freddie

   Snack Item: _____
   Price: _____
   Number of Coin Combinations: _____

2. Vicky

   Snack Item: _____
   Price: _____
   Number of Coin Combinations: _____

3. Danny

   Snack Item: _____
   Price: _____
   Number of Coin Combinations: _____

4. Mary

   Snack Item: _____
   Price: _____
   Number of Coin Combinations: _____

5. Eddie

   Snack Item: _____
   Price: _____
   Number of Coin Combinations: _____

Bonus Box: Create an organized list of coin combinations for the items not purchased by the friends above.

Doing the Two-Step

There's no need to dance around these problems if you know the steps to take!

Purpose: To solve word problems by identifying and using correct operations

Students will do the following:

- interpret clue words given
- add, subtract, multiply, and divide
- write an original two-step word problem

Materials for each student:

- copy of page 160
- pencil
- paper clip

Vocabulary to review:

- operations
- number sentence

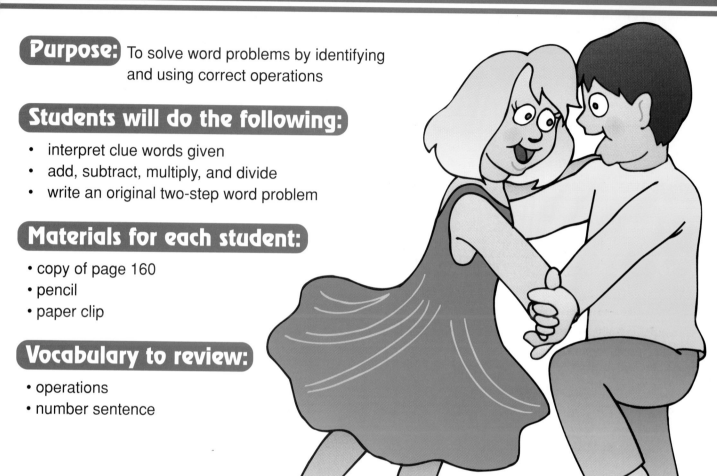

Extension activities to use after the reproducible:

- Give your students a mental workout with the following mental math game! Read aloud to your students the following equation: $10 \times 4 - 2 + 7 = \square$. Instruct each student to solve the equation in her head without using paper and pencil. Give your students a few more multistep problems to solve mentally; then have each student create her own multistep problem that contains two or three different operations. Next, select a student to read her problem aloud to the class. Instruct her to select another student to answer the problem. If the answer is correct, that student gets to read his problem to the class. Continue this process until each student has read his problem aloud to the class and/or answered another student's problem.

- See if your students are up to the challenge of solving the following equations. The problem is that the operation signs have been left out. Write each problem below on the board. Then have students work in pairs to correctly place the operation signs ($+$, $-$, $\times$, $\div$) back into each problem.

> **60567 = 34,020** ($60 \times 567 = 34{,}020$)
> **3921786 = 4,707** ($3{,}921 + 786 = 4{,}707$)
> **432176 = 256** ($432 - 176 = 256$)
> **132762 = 6,638** ($13{,}276 \div 2 = 6{,}638$)
> Challenge: The following problem is missing the operation sign and the equal sign.
> **902180** ($90 \times 2 = 180$)

Doing the Two-Step

Read each problem carefully. Then decide the 2 steps needed to solve the problem. Write the 2-step number sentence you will use to solve the problem in the blank provided; then solve it! Be careful! Sometimes the same operation will be used twice!

1. Sarah had $50.00 to spend on refreshments. She spent $17.85 for juice and another $30.50 for chips and salsa. How much money does she have left?

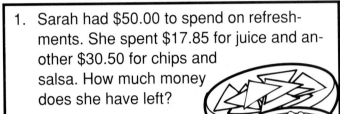

Answer:_____

2. Pat is making decorations for the dance. He filled 5 boxes each with 40 paper flowers. Then he made 37 foil bows. How many decorations has he made so far?

Answer:_____

3. Archie filled 120 cups with juice. He placed 15 cups on each tray. He accidentally spilled 3 trays of juice. How many trays of juice does he still have for the dance?

Answer:_____

4. Linda's mom brought 3 packs of cookies. Each pack has 4 rows of 10 cookies. How many cookies does she have all together?

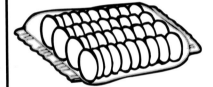

Answer:_____

5. The football game before the dance was attended by 3,000 people. It was raining, so 550 people left at halftime. Then 780 more people left after the third quarter. How many people were at the game when the fourth quarter started?

Answer:_____

6. Sandi has 8 pizzas with 6 slices in each. She served 40 slices of pizza at the refreshment table. How many slices were left over?

Answer:_____

7. Guests at the dance ate 4 boxes of chocolate chip cookies, each containing 20 cookies. They also ate 75 sugar cookies. How many cookies did they eat in all?

Answer:_____

8. The fund-raising committee sold 50 $2.00 raffle tickets and $25.00 worth of soda during the dance. How much money did they raise?

Answer:_____

Extra! Extra! Read All About It!

Have your students hit the beat and discover the word problems behind the headlines.

Purpose: To write word problems using a given topic and number sentence

Students will do the following:

- write multistep word problems

Materials for each student:

- copy of page 162
- pencil

Vocabulary for review:

- headline
- topic
- number sentence
- multistep problem

WHAT A SCOOP!

Extension activities to use after the reproducible:

- Combine your students' love of literature and problem solving with the following activity. Read a familiar fairy tale to your class, such as *Little Red Riding Hood.* Afterward, ask your students a couple of word problems that include characters and events from the story. For example: "Little Red Riding Hood filled a basket for her grandmother with 15 items. Along the way, she tripped and lost three items. Then, further along the trail, she dropped two more items. How many items did she have left when she arrived at her grandmother's house?" *(15 − 3 − 2 = 10)* Then select a new fairy tale to read aloud to the class. After reading the tale, instruct each student to write a two-step problem based on the fairy tale on a large index card. Collect the cards and combine them into a problem-solving book. Place the fairy tale and the student-made problem-solving book in a center for students to read and complete during their free time.

- Improve your students' writing and math skills with the following activity. Divide your students into small groups. Then assign each group one of the following themes: amusement park, dude ranch, water park, or rock concert. (Or you may want to assign each group a theme related to a topic you are currently studying.) Instruct each group to write four word problems for its assigned theme. Then have each group exchange problems with another group to solve.

Extra! Extra! Read All About It!

Read each headline and number sentence carefully. Then write a word problem that involves the headline's topic and can be solved by using the number sentence given. One has been done for you.

---

1. **Boy Buys Friends Hot Cocoa**

   Brad offered to buy cocoa for all his friends. First, 5 friends took him up on the offer. Then 3 more wanted cocoa too. If each drink cost $1.75, how much did Brad spend?

   Answer: (5 + 3) x $1.75 = $14.00

2. **Best Muffins in Town!**

   _____

   _____

   _____

   _____

   _____

   Answer: (12 ÷ 2) x $3.00 = $18.00

---

3. **Riders Try Out New Ski Lift**

   _____

   _____

   _____

   _____

   _____

   Answer: 200 − 75 + 37 = 162

4. **Huge Sale at Sports World**

   _____

   _____

   _____

   _____

   _____

   Answer: $50 − (4 x $8.99) = $14.04

---

5. **Mountain Rescue Team Succeeds!**

   _____

   _____

   _____

   _____

   Answer: (2 x 5) + (7 x 3) = 31

6. **Snowboarding Championship Held**

   _____

   _____

   _____

   _____

   Answer: (52 ÷ 4) + 8 = 21

---

7. **Concert Tickets Go on Sale**

   _____

   _____

   _____

   _____

   Answer: ($10 x 14) + ($20 x 20) = $540

8. **Need Piano Lessons?**

   _____

   _____

   _____

   Answer: (4 x 30 min.) + (4 x 60 min.) = 360 minutes = 6 hours

---

Bonus Box: On the back of this sheet, create your own multistep word problem for a friend to solve.

Use with the second extension activity on page 25, page 26, and the second extension activity on page 29.

Clock

Use with the first extension activity on page 53.

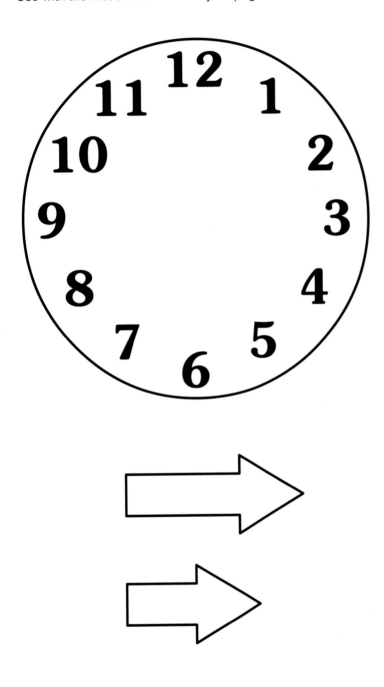

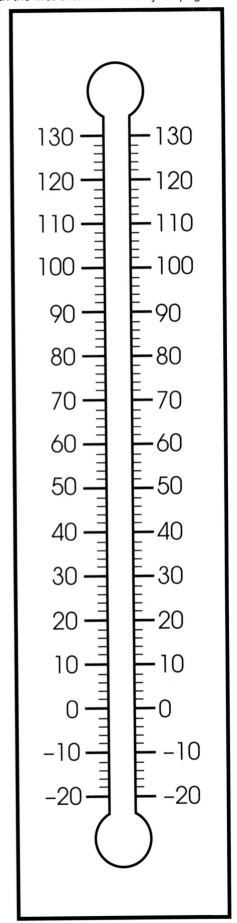

Use with the second extension activity on page 53.

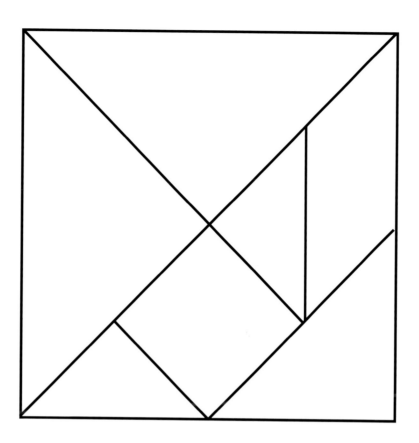

10 x 10 Grid

Use with the first extension activity on page 59, the first extension activity on page 65, and the first extension activity on page 97.

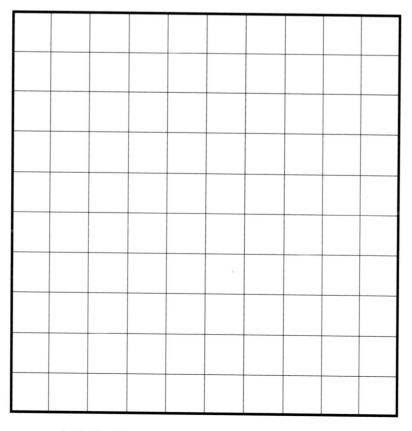

Hundreds Chart

Use with the first extension activity on page 131.

1	2	3	4	5	6	7	8	9	10
11	12	13	14	15	16	17	18	19	20
21	22	23	24	25	26	27	28	29	30
31	32	33	34	35	36	37	38	39	40
41	42	43	44	45	46	47	48	49	50
51	52	53	54	55	56	57	58	59	60
61	62	63	64	65	66	67	68	69	70
71	72	73	74	75	76	77	78	79	80
81	82	83	84	85	86	87	88	89	90
91	92	93	94	95	96	97	98	99	100

Cube

Use with the second extension activity on page 81, page 82, the
first extension activity on page 89, and page 94.

Directions for assembling the cube:
1. Label the pattern.
2. Cut out the pattern along the solid lines.
3. Fold along the dotted lines.
4. Paste, glue, or tape the sides together at the tabs.

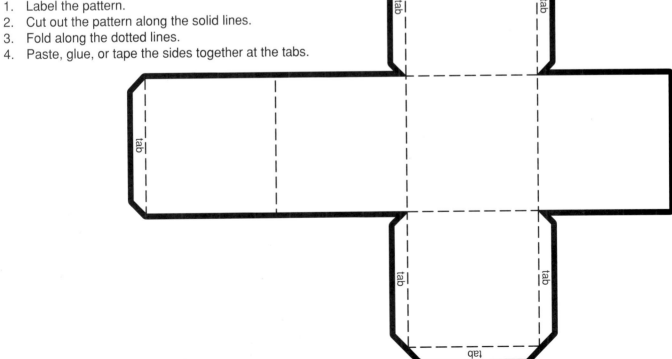

Answer Keys

Page 8

Answers for which items should be taken home or put in the trash may vary. Possible answers are shown below.

Book = $1\frac{7}{8}$

Barrette = $\frac{3}{4}$ or $\frac{6}{8}$ (Trash)

Bookmark = $2\frac{3}{4}$ or $2\frac{6}{8}$

Sandwich = $1\frac{3}{8}$ (Trash)

Comb = $1\frac{1}{8}$ (Trash)

Shoe = $1\frac{7}{8}$ (Trash)

Gum = $1\frac{1}{4}$ or $1\frac{2}{8}$ (Trash)

Mitten = $1\frac{1}{2}$ or $1\frac{2}{4}$ or $1\frac{4}{8}$ (Trash)

Bonus Box: Gum + Bookmark = 4; Comb + Shoe = 3; Barrette + Gum = 2

Page 10

Part I:

1. kilogram
2. milligram
3. kilogram
4. gram
5. gram
6. gram

Part II:

1. horseshoe: kg (P)
2. raindrop: mg (L)
3. picnic table: kg (E)
4. volleyball: g (A)
5. paper plate: g (S)
6. bottle of soda: kg (E)
7. bowl of potato salad: kg (L)
8. dash of pepper: mg (E)
9. bottle of ketchup: g (T)
10. hot dog: g (T)
11. piece of charcoal: g (U)
12. grill: kg (C)
13. softball: g (E)
14. wooden bat: kg (E)
15. dab of sunscreen: mg (A)
16. watermelon seed: mg (T)

Riddle:

P L E A S E   L E T T U C E   E A T !
1 2 3 4 5 6   7 8 9 10 11 12 13   14 15 16

Page 12

Part I:

Answers are from heaviest to lightest.

Gus: 35 ounces; 2 pounds, 2 ounces; 32 ounces; 25 ounces; 1 pound, 7 ounces; 12 ounces

Garth: 2 pounds, 1 ounce; 29 ounces; 1 pound, 10 ounces; 1 pound, 8 ounces; 18 ounces; 15 ounces

Gary: 1 pound, 10 ounces; 25 ounces; 1 pound, 5 ounces; 20 ounces; 16 ounces; 8 ounces

Gunther: 2 pounds, 2 ounces; 33 ounces; 27 ounces; 1 pound, 9 ounces; 23 ounces; 17 ounces

Part II:

1. **Gus:** 35 ounces; 2 pounds, 3 ounces
   Garth: 33 ounces; 2 pounds, 1 ounce
   Gary: 26 ounces; 1 pound, 10 ounces
   Gunther: 34 ounces; 2 pounds, 2 ounces

2. **Gus:** 12 ounces
   Garth: 15 ounces
   Gary: 8 ounces
   Gunther: 17 ounces

3. Gus is the winner.

Bonus Box:

Gus = 10 pounds, 1 ounce

Garth = 9 pounds, 1 ounce

Gary = 7 pounds, 4 ounces

Gunther = 9 pounds, 15 ounces

Page 14

1. 50 l
2. 200 ml
3. 450 ml
4. 10 l
5. 35 ml
6. 8 l

Bonus Box: 68 l; 685 ml

Page 16

1. 1 gallon = 4 quarts
2. $\frac{3}{4}$ quart = 3 cups
3. $\frac{1}{2}$ gallon = 4 pints
4. $3\frac{1}{2}$ pints = 7 cups
5. 20 cups = 5 quarts
6. 6 pints = 3 quarts
7. 8 cups = 4 pints
8. $\frac{1}{4}$ gallon = 4 cups
9. 8 quarts = 2 gallons
10. 10 pints = 5 quarts
11. 2 gallons = 16 pints
12. 5 pints = 3 cups
13. 3 quarts = 6 pints
14. $\frac{3}{4}$ gallon = 6 pints
15. 16 pints = 8 quarts
16. 32 cups = 2 gallons
17. 16 pints = 2 gallons
18. 9 quarts = 36 cups
19. 12 quarts = 3 gallons
20. 20 quarts = 5 gallons

Page 20

1. I
2. E
3. R
4. U
5. P
6. K
7. S
8. D

Riddle:

A   S U P E R   K I D
    7 4 5 2 3   6 1 8

Page 22

1. 6:35
2. 6:00
3. 7:25
4. 6:50
5. 6:10
6. 6:40
7. 6:55
8. 7:15
9. 7:15
10. 6:30

Molly believes the cakenapper is Missy Morton.

Bonus Box: Mike Mancini

Page 24

1. **Marvin:** 4 hrs. 7 mins., 7
2. **Maurice:** 3 hrs. 35 mins., 3
3. **Marty:** 3 hrs. 44 mins., 4
4. **Martha:** 3 hrs. 58 mins., 6
5. **Marie:** 3 hrs. 13 mins., 2
6. **Molly:** 2 hrs. 50 mins., 1
7. **Margo:** 3 hrs. 48 mins., 5
8. **Max:** 4 hrs. 39 mins., 8
9. **Mandi:** 4 hrs. 54 mins., 9
10. **Marcy:** 5 hrs. 6 mins., 10

Bonus Box: 8 hrs. 57 mins.

Page 28

1. 17 sq cm, 170 sq m
2. 17 sq cm, 170 sq m
3. 18 sq cm, 180 sq m
4. 10 sq cm, 100 sq m
5. 21 sq cm, 210 sq m
6. 16 sq cm, 160 sq m
7. 9 sq cm, 90 sq m

Bonus Box: 1,080 sq m

Page 30
1. 28 sq cm
2. 45 sq cm
3. 25 sq cm
4. 27 sq cm
5. 18 sq cm

6. 15 sq cm
7. 22 sq cm
8. 32 sq cm
9. 12 sq cm
10. 20 sq cm

Blueprint designs will vary.

Bonus Box:
elephants, cheetahs, zebras, monkeys, hyenas, antelope, rhinos, birds, lions, crocodiles; Word problems will vary.

Page 40
1. 5 cm
2. 15°C
3. 50 g
4. 1 l
5. 360 m
6. 4,500 sq cm
7. 1 hr. 37 mins.
8. Answers will vary.

Page 32

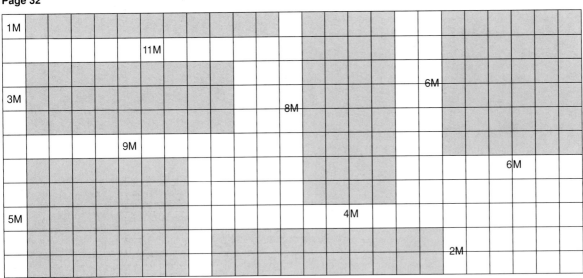

Bonus Box: Answers will vary.

Page 34
1. $4\frac{1}{2}$ in.
2. 7 in.
3. $4\frac{1}{2}$ in.
4. $6\frac{1}{2}$ in.
5. 6 in.
6. $6\frac{1}{2}$ in.
7. $6\frac{1}{2}$ in.
8. $5\frac{1}{2}$ in.

Bonus Box: 5.88 in.

Page 36
1. Perimeter; 140 ft.
2. Area; 1,000 tiles
3. Area; 625 sq. ft.
4. Perimeter; 220 ft.
5. Perimeter; 120 ft.
6. Area; No, the crew will be 375 sq. ft. short.

Bonus Box: $3,000

Page 38
1. $1\frac{1}{2}$ in.
2. $2\frac{1}{2}$ in.
3. Answers will vary.
4. 128 sq. ft.
5. 100 feet of fence
6. 3 lb.
7. 39 oz.
8. 3 lb.
9. 11 pt.
10. 9 gal.
11. 80 c.
12. 85°F
13. 32°F
14. 78°F
15. 9:55 A.M.
16. 6:25 A.M.
17. 5 hrs. 35 mins.

Page 42
(Note: The wall contains shapes that are not regular polygons and should not be colored.) Shapes that should be colored include

30   yellow triangles
19   green squares
7   blue pentagons
4   orange hexagons
6   red octagons
3   purple decagons

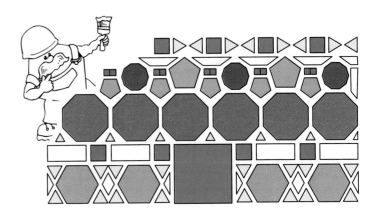

Page 44
Designs will vary. Accept any designs that meet the requirements described on page 44.

Page 46
Task #1:
Square—definitions 1, 2, 3, 4
Rectangle—definitions 1, 3
Rhombus—definitions 1, 2
Parallelogram—definition 1
Trapezoid—definition 5

Task #2:
a. True
b. False
c. False
d. True
e. True

Task #3: Answers will vary. Accept any reasonable response that basically states that a square is also a rectangle because it contains four 90° angles, but that not all rectangles are squares.

Page 48
1.

Space Figure	Name	Number of Faces	Number of Vertices	Sum of Faces and Vertices	Number of Edges
	Cube	6	8	14	12
	Rectangular Prism	6	8	14	12
	Triangular Prism	5	6	11	9
	Square Pyramid	5	5	10	8
	Rectangular Pyramid	5	5	10	8
	Triangular Pyramid	4	4	8	6

2. 2; yes
3. The sum of the faces and vertices for each space figure above is 2 more than the total number of edges for each space figure.

Bonus Box: Yes

Page 50
1. $\overleftrightarrow{AF}$ // $\overleftrightarrow{BE}$
2. $\overline{KL}$ // $\overline{HI}$; $\overline{FK}$ // $\overline{BI}$; $\overline{EF}$ // $\overline{AB}$; $\overline{AL}$ // $\overline{EH}$
3. Answers may vary. Possible answers include the following:
   $\overleftrightarrow{AG} \bowtie \overleftrightarrow{AF}$; $\overleftrightarrow{BE} \bowtie \overleftrightarrow{MN}$; $\overleftrightarrow{AG} \bowtie \overleftrightarrow{BE}$; $\overleftrightarrow{AG} \bowtie \overleftrightarrow{MN}$; $\overleftrightarrow{AF} \bowtie \overleftrightarrow{MN}$
4. $\overrightarrow{DH}$
5. Answers may vary. Possible answers include the following:
   $\overleftrightarrow{BE} \perp \overleftrightarrow{MN}$; $\overleftrightarrow{AF} \perp \overleftrightarrow{MN}$
6. Answers will vary. Accept any reasonable illustration.

Page 52
1. haven't (10°)
2. heard (80°)
3. I'm (130°)
4. feathered (30°)
5. bird (50°)
6. rainbow (140°)
7. colors (70°)
8. see (150°)
9. doesn't (90°)
10. everyone (40°)
11. be (170°)
12. me (100°)

Page 54
A: 105°, obtuse
B: 100°, obtuse
C: 73°, acute
D: 90°, right
E: 130°, obtuse
F: 140°, obtuse
G: 70°, acute
H: 90°, right
I: 20°, acute
J: 109°, obtuse
K: 40°, acute

Page 56
2.
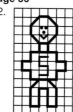

3.
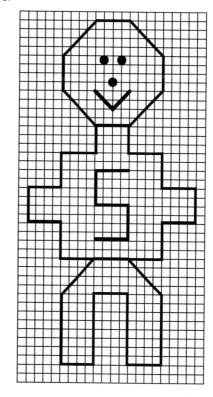

Bonus Box: Answers will vary.

Page 58:
Part I:
Wedges 2, 4, and 6 are congruent to the one held by Marvin.

Part II:

$\overline{AC}$	≅	$\overline{KL}$	$\overline{BA}$	≅	$\overline{JK}$	$\overline{NQ}$	≅	$\overline{IG}$
∠BCA	≅	∠JLK	$\overline{OM}$	≅	$\overline{ED}$	∠ONQ	≅	∠EIG
∠DHG	≅	∠MRQ	$\overline{CE}$	≅	$\overline{LO}$	$\overline{BF}$	≅	$\overline{JP}$
∠OPR	≅	∠EFH	∠JLK	≅	∠BCA	$\overline{KR}$	≅	$\overline{AH}$

Part III:
Students' drawings of the wedge of cheese should vary only slightly from the original. The length of the line segments and the measure of the angles should match the original as closely as possible.

Bonus Box: Answers will vary.

Page 60

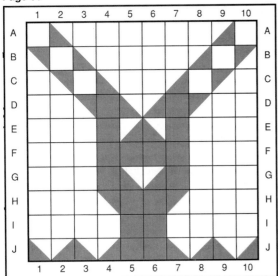

Page 64
1. slide
2. flip
3. slide
4. flip
5. turn
6. turn
7. slide
8. flip
9. turn

Page 76
1. Popsicle®, PUSH UP® pop, ice-cream cone, Italian ice
2. Popsicle: 3 out of 8 $(\frac{3}{8})$
   PUSH UP pop: 2 out of 8 $(\frac{2}{8})$
   ice-cream cone: 1 out of 8 $(\frac{1}{8})$
   Italian ice: 2 out of 8 $(\frac{2}{8})$
3. most likely: Popsicle
   least likely: ice-cream cone
   equally likely: PUSH UP pop and Italian ice
4. Students' answers will vary. To make a prediction, students should multiply the probability by the number of spins.
   Popsicle: $\frac{3}{8}$ x 20 = about 8 times
   PUSH UP pop: $\frac{2}{8}$ x 20 = 5 times
   ice-cream cone: $\frac{1}{8}$ x 20 = about 3 times
   Italian ice: $\frac{2}{8}$ x 20 = 5 times
5. Answers will vary.
6. Answers will vary.

Page 78
1. First Place: 90–99, Second Place: 80–89, Third Place: 70–79, Fourth Place: 60–69, Honorable Mention: 50–59
2.

Place	Interval	Tally	Frequency
First	90–99	﬩	5
Second	80–89	IIII	4
Third	70–79	﬩ IIII	9
Fourth	60–69	﬩ III	8
Honorable Mention	50–59	﬩ II	7

3. 8
4. 33
5. 5 more
6. Harry is most likely to award a third place ribbon because there are more scores in this category than in any other. Harry is least likely to award a second place ribbon because there are fewer scores in this category than in any other.

Page 66

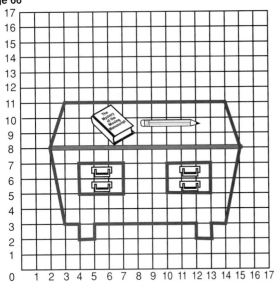

The missing manuscript was last seen on Miss MacChristie's
___desk___.

Where was the missing manuscript found?
in the D E S K   D R A W E R
(7, 9) (1, 1) (1, 8) (8, 5)   (7, 9) (9, 7) (4, 4) (1, 4) (1, 1) (9, 7)

Page 72
Part I:
Have student partners exchange garden scenes and measure the items in each other's scenes. Remind students that the radius of a circle is half of its diameter—and that the diameter of a circle is two times its radius.

Part II:
a. 24 inches; since the radius is 12 inches, the diameter is 2 times 12, or 24.
b. 7 centimeters; since the diameter is 14 centimeters, the radius is half of 14, or 7.
c. Answers will vary.
d. 25.12 centimeters
e. Answers will vary.

Bonus Box: The circle with a radius of 5 cm has a greater circumference since its diameter is 10 cm.

Page 80
1.

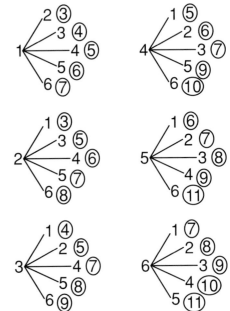

2. 30 possible outcomes
3. $\frac{22}{30}$
4. $\frac{8}{30}$

Bonus Box: Twelve additional outcomes are possible.

Page 82

Part I: Game results and students' answers will vary.

Part II:

	1	2	3	4	5	6
1	1	②	3	④	5	⑥
2	②	④	⑥	⑧	⑩	⑫
3	3	⑥	9	⑫	15	⑱
4	④	⑧	⑫	⑯	⑳	㉔
5	5	⑩	15	⑳	25	㉚
6	⑥	⑫	⑱	㉔	㉚	㊱

1. Based on the product table, an even product is more likely to be rolled. There are 27 even products and only 9 odd products.
2. Based on the information in the product table, the game is not fair. There is a more likely chance of rolling an even product.

Bonus Box: Rolling an odd or even number would be equally likely because there are the same number of odd and even numbers on a number cube (3 of each).

Page 84

1. red, red; red, blue; red, green
   blue, red; blue, blue; blue, green
   green, red; green, blue; green, green
2. There are 9 possible outcomes. The probability of spinning a match with the 2 spinners is 3 out of 9, or $\frac{3}{9}$. The probability of spinning a mismatch with the 2 spinners is 6 out of 9, or $\frac{6}{9}$.
3. Answers will vary.
4. Player 2 should be chosen. There are more chances to spin a mismatch.
5. Students' letters should state that the president should not sell the game because it is not fair. There is not an equally likely chance of spinning both a match and a mismatch.

Bonus Box: If the colors on the spinners were changed to those shown, Player 1 would still not have a more likely chance of winning the game. The probability of his spinning a match would only be $\frac{4}{9}$, while the probability of Player 2 spinning a mismatch would be $\frac{5}{9}$.

Page 88

	Oatmeal Raisin	Chocolate Chip	Sugar	Peanut Butter	Mint	Mean	Median	Mode	Range
Minnie	8	15	10	5	12	10	10	–	10
Marty	4	10	13	7	16	10	10	–	12
Molly	7	4	8	8	13	8	8	8	9
Michael	8	8	15	8	6	9	8	8	9
Milton	6	11	7	7	9	8	7	7	5
Monty	6	20	13	9	12	12	12	–	14
Mandy	7	18	10	13	7	11	10	7	11
Mabel	6	16	5	8	5	8	6	5	11
Mary	3	8	6	6	2	5	6	6	6
Merwin	5	10	13	9	8	9	9	–	8

1. Monty
2. Mary
3. Minnie and Marty—10; Molly, Milton, and Mabel—8; Michael and Merwin—9
4. Mandy
5. 8
6. 7
7. 9
8. Mabel

Bonus Box: Chocolate chip had the highest mean in number of boxes sold *(12)*. Oatmeal raisin had the lowest mean in number of boxes sold *(6)*.

Page 92

1. Twizzlers® *(26 grams)* have less sugar than Starburst® *(32 grams)*.
2. M&M's® *(31 grams)* have more sugar than Snickers® *(29 grams)*.
3. Ten more grams of sugar are in a Snickers *(29 grams)* than in a Reese's® *(19 grams)*.
4. M&M's = 31 grams, Reese's = 19 grams, Snickers = 29 grams, Starburst = 32 grams, Twizzlers = 26 grams
5. 137 total grams of sugar
6. Reese's *(19 grams)*, Twizzlers *(26 grams)*, Snickers *(29 grams)*, M&M's *(31 grams)*, Starburst *(32 grams)*

Bonus Box: About 27 grams

Page 96

1. 80 bicycles
2. Thursday
3. 70 more bicycles
4. 200 − 160 = 40
5. more
6. $1,900
7. No, he only rented 1,020 this week.
8. 200 + 190 + 160 = 550
9. Tuesday
10. 146 bicycles

Bonus Box:
Sunday = 80, Monday = 55, Tuesday = 40, Wednesday = 65, Thursday = 75, Friday = 100, Saturday = 95

Page 98

1. JOHN HENRY
2. PINOCCHIO
3. FROG PRINCE
4. SNOW WHITE
5. IKTOMI
6. PECOS BILL
7. ANANSI
8. RAPUNZEL

Bonus Box:
Cinderella—(9, 9) (3, 7) (7, 8) (4, 1) (6, 2) (5, 3) (6, 2) (6, 5) (6, 5) (4, 4)
Goldilocks—(1, 4) (4, 6) (6, 5) (4, 1) (3, 7) (6, 5) (4, 6) (9, 9) (7, 4) (1, 9)
Aladdin—(4, 4) (6, 5) (4, 4) (4, 1) (4, 1) (3, 7) (7, 8)
Hansel & Gretel—(3, 9) (4, 4) (7, 8) (1, 9) (6, 2) (6, 5) & (1, 4) (5, 3) (6, 2) (9, 5) (6, 2) (6, 5)

Page 100

1. week 1
2. week 1
3. week 3
4. August
5. August; week 4
6. 275
7. weeks 2 and 3; 100 tickets
8. 3
9. 300
10. 313

Bonus Box: Answers will vary. One possible answer: Ticket sales may have increased as people had their last bit of fun before the school year started.

Page 102

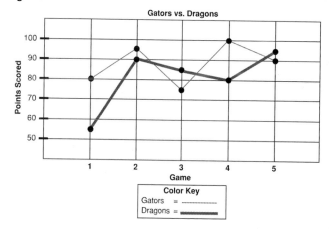

1. Gators
2. Dragons, 10 points
3. 81
4. 88
5. 2
6. Game 4
7. 5 points
8. Game 1

Page 104
1. clothing store—$32.00
2. movie rental store—$8.00
3. $16.00
4. 70%
5. $16.00
6. music—$36.00, clothes—$48.00, candy—$24.00, movies—$12.00

Page 106
A.

Potato	Frequency	Fraction	Percentage
mashed	20	$\frac{20}{50} = \frac{40}{100}$	40%
baked	5	$\frac{5}{50} = \frac{10}{100}$	10%
fried	15	$\frac{15}{50} = \frac{30}{100}$	30%
chips	10	$\frac{10}{50} = \frac{20}{100}$	20%

B.

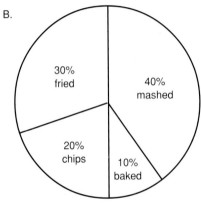

C. Answers will vary.

Page 108
B. least to greatest order:
22, 23, 28, 33, 36, 37, 40, 46, 48, 49, 51, 51, 51, 54, 54, 55, 58, 60, 65, 68, 79

Teen Tournament Scores

```
2 | 2 3 8
3 | 3 6 7
4 | 0 6 8 9
5 | 1 1 1 4 4 5 8
6 | 0 5 8
7 | 9
```

Key: 2/2 represents a score of 22

1. 48
2. 51
3. 51
4. 57

Bonus Box: mean: 59; median: 56; mode: 88; range: 63

Page 110
Explanations may vary.
1. C; Each part of the circle graph is equal.
2. D; Three bars represent each type of recyclable material.
3. A; The line graph shows a steady increase.
4. F; The pictograph has 7 rows of data; each row represents 1 of the 7 continents.
5. E; One section of the circle graph represents more than 50 percent.
6. B; The line graph starts out high, then decreases.
7. H; Two of the bars are equal, representing the equal votes won by basketball and soccer.
8. G; Row 1 shows twice as many as row 2.

Bonus Box: Answers will vary.

Page 112
1. property of one
2. commutative property
3. property of one, 362
4. zero property
5. distributive property
6. associative property, (2 x 3) x 4 = 6 x 4 = 24
7. property of one, 17
8. associative property
9. zero property, 0
10. commutative property, 4 x 12 = 48
11. zero property, 0
12. commutative property, 4 x 63 = 252
13. associative property
14. distributive property
15. distributive property, (50 x 9) + (8 x 9) = 450 + 72 = 522

Page 114
1. 35, 45, 55, 65
2. 9, 10, 11, 12
3. 32, 10, 15, 56
4. 9, 20, 23, 18
5. 3, 28, 5, 49
6. 16, 11, 15, 20
7. 35, 56, 11, 15
8. 18, 20, 11, 17

Bonus Box: 48, 60, 72, 96

Page 116
1. y = x + 1 or x = y − 1
2. y = x + 4 or x = y − 4
3. y = 5x or x = y ÷ 5
4. y = 2x or x = y ÷ 2

Answers for problems 5–8 will vary. Possible answers:
5. (1, 3), (2, 4), (3, 5), (4, 6), (5, 7)
6. (1, 4), (2, 5), (3, 6), (4, 7), (5, 8)
7. (1, 2), (2, 4), (3, 6), (4, 8), (5, 10)
8. (3, 7), (4, 6), (5, 5), (6, 4), (7, 3)

Bonus Box: Answers will vary. One possible answer: (1, 5), (2, 7), (3, 9), (4, 11), (5, 13).

Page 118
1. y = 5, 6, 7, 8, 9
   The graphed ordered pairs are (2, 5), (3, 6), (4, 7), (5, 8), and (6, 9).

2. y = 2, 6, 10, 14, 18
   The graphed ordered pairs are (1, 2), (3, 6), (5, 10), (7, 14), and (9, 18).

3. y = 8, 10, 12, 14, 16
   The graphed ordered pairs are (16, 8), (20, 10), (24, 12), (28, 14), and (32, 16).

Bonus Box: y = 7, 8, 9, 10, 11
The graphed ordered pairs are (2, 7), (3, 8), (4, 9), (5, 10), and (6, 11).

Page 120
1. 5
2. 4
3. 18
4. 23
5. 31
6. 32
7. 6
8. 11
9. 63
10. 8
11. 48
12. 66
13. 86
14. 12
15. 7
16. 17

Riddle: A STICKY SITUATION

Bonus Box: Answers vary.

Page 122
Answers may vary. Suggested answers include the following:
1. n − 5 ≤ 36
2. 7n < 49
3. 24 ÷ n ≤ 6
4. n − 7 ≤ 12
5. 4n + 7 ≤ 28
6. 27 + n < 40
7. 7n + 3 ≤ 25
8. 9n ≤ 52

Bonus Box: The groups could range in size from 2 to 12 people. Students' explanations of how they got their answers will vary.

Page 124

1. $3x = 51$
2. $x - 18 = 14$
3. $12 \div x = 3$ or $12 \div 3 = x$
4. $x + 2 = 15$
5. $24 - x = 16$
6. $4x - \$3.00 = \$9.00$
7. $\$10.00 \div x = \$2.00$ or $2x = 10$
8. $2x + \$5.00 = \$9.00$

Bonus Box: $17.00

Page 126

1. −10 feet, 10 feet
2. 40 feet
3. 190 feet
4. −30 feet
5. −50 feet

Bonus Box: Answers will vary.

Page 128

1. Laura = 4 events *(given in problem)*
   Susie = 16 events *(4 x 4)*
   Chelsea = 22 events *(16 + 6)*
   Ben = 8 events *(16 ÷ 2)*

   Answer: 8 events

2. Week 1: $23.10 *(given in problem)*
   Week 2: $36.90 *($23.10 + $13.80)*
   Week 3: $28.15 *($36.90 − $8.75)*
   Week 4: $56.30 *($28.15 x 2)*

   Answer: $56.30

3. Lindsey = 4 back flips *(given in problem)*
   Lisa = 2 back flips *(4 ÷ 2)*
   Larry = 4 back flips *(2 + 2)*
   Liz = 12 back flips *(3 x 4)*

   Answer: 12 back flips

4. 6:00 P.M. − 45 minutes = 5:15 P.M.
   5:15 P.M. − 40 minutes = 4:35 P.M.
   4:35 P.M. − 60 minutes = 3:35 P.M.
   3:35 P.M. − 35 minutes = 3:00 P.M.

   Answer: 3:00 p.m.

5. Balance beam = 15 gymnasts *(given in problem)*
   Floor mats = 15 gymnasts*
   Uneven bars = 15 gymnasts*
   Vault = 45 gymnasts

   *Balance beam, floor mats, and uneven bars had equal amounts of students. The problem states there were 15 gymnasts at the balance beam, so there should also be 15 at the floor mats and 15 at the uneven bars.

   Answer: 90 gymnasts *(45 + 15 + 15 + 15 = 90)*

Bonus Box:

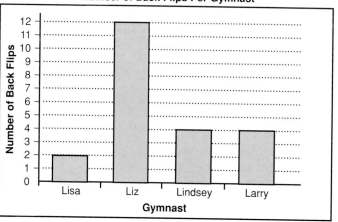

Number of Back Flips Per Gymnast

Page 130

1. Soccer ball = $19.95 *(given in problem)*
   Pair of sneakers = $59.85 *($19.95 x 3)*
   Money left after purchases = $7.80 *(given in problem)*

   Answer: $87.60 *($19.95 + $59.85 + $7.80 = $87.60)*

2. Shake = $2.50 *(given in problem)*
   Sub and soda = $5.00 *($2.50 x 2)*
   Fries = $2.99 *(given in problem)*
   Money left after purchases = $3.10 *(given in problem)*

   Answer: $13.59
   ($2.50 + $5.00 + $2.99 + $3.10 = $13.59)

3. Amount of money at end of shift = $540.12 *(given in problem)*
   Customer #1 $129.99 *(given in problem)*
   Customer #2 $259.98 *($129.99 x 2)*
   Customer #3 $50.00 *(given in problem)*

   Answer: $100.03
   ($540.00 − $129.99 − $259.98 − $50.00 = $100.03)

4. Cindi = $102.04 *(given in problem)*
   Curt = $306.12 *($102.04 x 3)*
   William = $153.06 *($306.12 ÷ 2)*
   Money DJ had left to give away = $102.04 *(given in problem)*

   Answer: $663.26
   ($102.04 + $153.06 + $306.12 + $102.04 = $663.26)

5. Amount of money left = $2.10 *(given in problem)*
   Movie ticket = $4.25 *(given in problem)*
   Drink = $1.75 *(given in problem)*
   Poster = $3.90 *(given in problem)*

   Answer: $12.00
   ($3.90 + $1.75 + $4.25 + 2.10 = $12.00)

6. Hat = $10.00 *(given in problem)*
   Scarf = $5.00 *($10.00 ÷ 2)*
   Blouse = $15.00 *(3 x $5.00)*

   Answer: $15.00

Bonus Box: No. Kathy only has $7.80 left from her purchases in problem 1. The 3 barrettes cost $8.25 *($2.25 x 3 = $8.25)*. She would need an extra $.45 to buy the 3 barrettes.

Page 132

1. Benny—sausage, Bobby—chopped beef, Barbara—sliced beef, Betty—ribs, Biff—chicken
2. Betty—lemonade, Barbara—fruit punch, Benny—soda, Bobby—chocolate shake, Biff—water
3. Benny—barbecued beans, Bobby—corn, Barbara—tossed salad, Betty—hush puppies, Biff—french fries
4. Benny—apple pie, Bobby—blackberry cobbler, Barbara—strawberry pie, Betty—chocolate delight, Biff—ice cream

Page 134

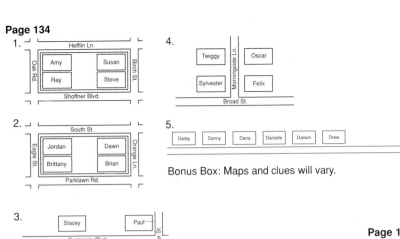

1. (map: Hefflin Ln., Oak Rd., Birch St., Shoffner Blvd. — Amy, Susan, Ray, Steve)
4. (map: Morningside Ln., Broad St. — Twiggy, Oscar, Sylvester, Felix)

2. (map: South St., Eagle St., Orange Ln., Parklawn Rd. — Jordan, Dawn, Brittany, Brian)

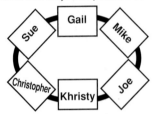

5. Darby, Danny, Dana, Danielle, Darwin, Drew

3. (map: Sunnyway Blvd., Parker St. — Stacey, Paul, Ed, Shawn, Nancy, Sherri)

Bonus Box: Maps and clues will vary.

Page 136

1. Answer can vary. One possible solution:

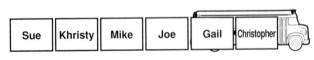

(circle: Sue, Gail, Mike, Christopher, Khristy, Joe)

2. Answer can vary. One possible solution:

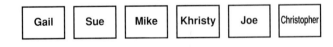

(Christopher, Joe, Gail, Khristy, Mike, Sue)

3.

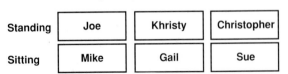

Sue | Khristy | Mike | Joe | Gail | Christopher

4.

Gail | Sue | Mike | Khristy | Joe | Christopher

5. Answer can vary. One possible solution:

Standing	Joe	Khristy	Christopher
Sitting	Mike	Gail	Sue

Page 138

1. Pencil: $0.40; Eraser: $0.65
2. Binder: $5.50; Pencil pouch: $3.50
3. Folder: $0.80; Pen: $0.50
4. Protractor: $1.80; Compass: $2.40
5. Loose-leaf paper: $0.70; Notebook: $1.10
6. Pencil sharpener: $1.45; Ruler: $0.90

Bonus Box: The total cost would be $19.70.

Page 140

10 points: 45
20 points: 55
30 points: 64
40 points: 127
50 points: 242
60 points: 846
70 points: 1,221
80 points: 1,575
90 points: 1,002

Bonus Box: Answers and clues will vary. Possible clues include odd number, divisible by 5, sum of digits is 6, 3-digit number, third digit is greater than first 2 digits, etc.

Page 142

1. **Solution:** The song will be requested 32 times on the tenth day.

Day	1	2	3	4	5	6	7	8	9	10
Requests	5	12	10	17	15	22	20	27	25	32

2. **Solution:** Dan and Derek will work together 3 days during the 2-week period and 6 days during the 4-week period.

Day	S	M	T	W	TH	F	S	S	M	T	W	TH	F	S
Dan	x		x		x		x		x		x		x	
Derek			x				x	x			x		x	x

3. **Solution:** There were 740 CDs given away during the 10-day contest.

Day	1	2	3	4	5	6	7	8	9	10
CDs	20	32	44	56	68	80	92	104	116	128

4. **Solution:** There would be 40 hip-hop music fans.

Alternative	5	10	15	20	25
Hip-Hop	8	16	24	32	40

5. **Solution:** The prize is worth $120.

Day	1	2	3	4	5	6	7	8
Cash	$15	$30	$45	$60	$75	$90	$105	$120

Page 144

1. **Solution:** Three park visitors rode both the roller coaster and the wild water ride.

Visitors	1	2	3	4	5	6	7	8	9	10	11	12	13	14	15	16	17	18
Roller Coaster			x			x			x			x			x			x
Water Ride						x						x						x

2. **Solution:** Twenty-seven hot dogs and 18 fries were sold.

Hamburgers	7	14	21	28	35	42	49	56	63
Hot Dogs	3	6	9	12	15	18	21	24	27
Fries	2	4	6	8	10	12	14	16	18

3. **Solution:** Only 1 player won all 3 games.

Visitors	1	2	3	4	5	6	7	8	9	10	11	12	13	14	15	16	17	18	19	20	21	22	23	24	25	26	27	28	29	30
Softball Pitch					x					x					x					x					x					x
Dart Throw					x					x					x					x					x					x
Ring Toss															x															x

4. **Solution:** Dolly will jump through 75 hoops during the tenth week.

Week	1	2	3	4	5	6	7	8	9	10
Hoops	12	19	26	33	40	47	54	61	68	75

5. **Solution:** Three park visitors wore both sunglasses and a hat.

Visitors	1	2	3	4	5	6	7	8	9	10	11	12	13	14	15	16	17	18	19	20	21	22	23	24
Sunglasses				x				x				x				x				x				x
Hat								x								x								x

Page 146

1. 5 miles north

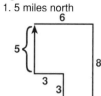

2. 8 planets

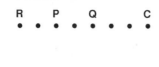

3. 13 doors

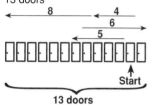

4. 20 kilometers south

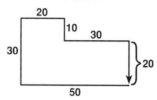

5. 13 stores

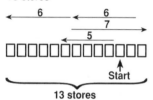

6. 4 miles west

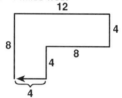

Bonus Box:
1. 28 miles
4. 160 kilometers

Page 148

1. Kathy is celebrating her 12th birthday.

2. She will need 4 or 5 tables.

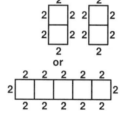

3. Each guest will receive 1 bar.

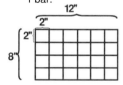

4. He will make 4 cuts.

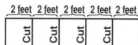

5. Four cookies will have chocolate chips and raisins, and 1 cookie will have chocolate chips, raisins, and nuts.

Bonus Box: Answers may vary. One possible solution:
She can make 3 evenly spaced cuts along the 8-inch side of the pan and 6 evenly spaced cuts along the 12-inch side of the pan to create 28 bars.

Page 150

1. Answer: 36 apples
   Pattern: add 6 apples and 1 basket
2. Answer: 75 apples
   Pattern: add 2 pies and 15 apples
3. Answer: 12 jars of apple jelly, 20 jars of apple butter
   Pattern: add 3 jars of apple jelly and 5 jars of apple butter
4. Answer: 45 apples
   Pattern: subtract 15, add 5
5. Answer: 30 muffins and 24 quarts of applesauce
   Pattern: add 6 muffins and 6 quarts of applesauce

Bonus Box: 320 apples

Page 152

1. 12 combinations, 3 combinations, 4 combinations

2. 6 combinations, 2 combinations

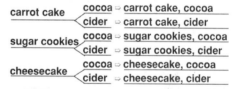

3. 6 combinations, 3 combinations

4. 18 different ways

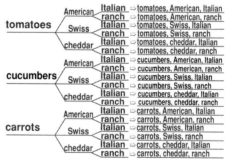

5. 18 meals, 6 include nacho chips

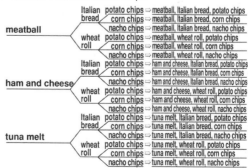

Bonus Box: 8 combinations

Page 154

1.
   - Fourteen are sprinters.
   - Three competed in all 3 events.
   - Fourteen competed in just 1 event.

2.
   - One competed in all 3 events.
   - Seven competed in both the javelin and discus, but not the shotput.
   - One competed in just the discus.

   Shotput / Javelin / Discus Venn diagram: Shotput top with 6; Javelin–Shotput overlap 4; Shotput–Discus overlap 3; center 1; Javelin only 5; Javelin–Discus overlap 7; Discus only 1.

3.
   - Five won all 3 medals.
   - Three won just a gold medal.
   - Six won just a silver medal.

   Gold / Bronze / Silver Venn diagram: Gold top with 3; Gold–Bronze overlap 3; Gold–Silver overlap 4; center 5; Bronze only 7; Bronze–Silver overlap 0; Silver only 6.

4.
   - Four ran in both the 100- and 200-yard dash, but not the 50-yard dash.
   - One ran in both the 50-yard and 200-yard dash, but not the 100-yard dash.
   - Seven ran in just the 50-yard dash.

   50-yard dash / 200-yard dash / 100-yard dash Venn diagram: 50-yard dash top with 7; overlaps 1 and 1; center 1; 200-yard only 4; overlap 4; 100-yard only 4.

Bonus Box:
18 sprinters; 7 competed in all 3 events; 14 competed in just 1 event

Page 156

1. 6 possible combinations

   ham, wheat
   ham, rye

   roastbeef, wheat
   roastbeef, rye

   turkey, wheat
   turkey, rye

2. 9 possible combinations

   ravioli, tomato
   ravioli, cream
   ravioli, pesto

   macaroni, tomato
   macaroni, cream
   macaroni, pesto

   spaghetti, tomato
   spaghetti, cream
   spaghetti, pesto

3. 10 possible combinations

   sundae, pudding
   sundae, toffee
   sundae, pie
   sundae, sorbet

   pudding, toffee
   pudding, pie
   pudding, sorbet

   toffee, pie
   toffee, sorbet

   pie, sorbet

4. 18 possible combinations

   ravioli, tomato, mozzarella
   ravioli, tomato, Romano
   ravioli, cream, mozzarella
   ravioli, cream, Romano
   ravioli, pesto, mozzarella
   ravioli, pesto, Romano

   macaroni, tomato, mozzarella
   macaroni, tomato, Romano
   macaroni, cream, mozzarella
   macaroni, cream, Romano
   macaroni, pesto, mozzarella
   macaroni, pesto, Romano

   spaghetti, tomato, mozzarella
   spaghetti, tomato, Romano
   spaghetti, cream, mozzarella
   spaghetti, cream, Romano
   spaghetti, pesto, mozzarella
   spaghetti, pesto, Romano

5. 27 possible combinations

   pita, salad, tea
   pita, salad, cola
   pita, salad, milk
   pita, rice, tea
   pita, rice, cola
   pita, rice, milk
   pita, soup, tea
   pita, soup, cola
   pita, soup, milk

   croissant, salad, tea
   croissant, salad, cola
   croissant, salad, milk
   croissant, rice, tea
   croissant, rice, cola
   croissant, rice, milk
   croissant, soup, tea
   croissant, soup, cola
   croissant, soup, milk

   enchilada, salad, tea
   enchilada, salad, cola
   enchilada, salad, milk
   enchilada, rice, tea
   enchilada, rice, cola
   enchilada, rice, milk
   enchilada, soup, tea
   enchilada, soup, cola
   enchilada, soup, milk

Bonus Box: combinations with peanut butter = 9; combinations with tea = 9; combinations with salad and tea = 3

Page 158

30¢

Q	D	N
1	0	1
0	3	0
0	2	2
0	1	4
0	0	6

Total Number of Coin Combinations = 5

35¢

Q	D	N
1	1	0
1	0	2
0	3	1
0	2	3
0	1	5
0	0	7

Total Number of Coin Combinations = 6

40¢

Q	D	N
1	1	1
1	0	3
0	4	0
0	3	2
0	2	4
0	1	6
0	0	8

Total Number of Coin Combinations = 7

45¢

Q	D	N
1	2	0
1	1	2
1	0	4
0	4	1
0	3	3
0	2	5
0	1	7
0	0	9

Total Number of Coin Combinations = 8

50¢

Q	D	N
2	0	0
1	2	1
1	1	3
1	0	5
0	5	0
0	4	2
0	3	4
0	2	6
0	1	8
0	0	10

Total Number of Coin Combinations = 10

55¢

Q	D	N
2	0	1
1	3	0
1	2	2
1	1	4
1	0	6
0	5	1
0	4	3
0	3	5
0	2	7
0	1	9
0	0	11

Total Number of Coin Combinations = 11

65¢

Q	D	N
2	1	1
2	0	3
1	4	0
1	3	2
1	2	4
1	1	6
1	0	8
0	6	1
0	5	3
0	4	5
0	3	7
0	2	9
0	1	11
0	0	13

Total Number of Coin Combinations = 14

75¢

Q	D	N
3	0	0
2	2	1
2	1	3
2	0	5
1	5	0
1	4	2
1	3	4
1	2	6
1	1	8
1	0	10
0	7	1
0	6	3
0	5	5
0	4	7
0	3	9
0	2	11
0	1	13
0	0	15

Total Number of Coin Combinations = 18

Page 160

Equations may vary.
1. $50.00 − ($17.85 + $30.50) = $1.65
2. (5 x 40) + 37 = 237 decorations
3. (120 ÷ 15) − 3 = 5 trays
4. 3 x (4 x 10) = 120 cookies
5. 3,000 − 550 − 780 = 1,670 people
6. (8 x 6) − 40 = 8 slices
7. (4 x 20) + 75 = 155 cookies
8. (50 x $2.00) + $25.00 = $125.00

Page 162

Students' word problems will vary. Accept any reasonable word problems.
Bonus Box: Answers will vary.